# WITHIN LIVING MEMORY
# THE WEST MIDLANDS

# WITHIN LIVING MEMORY

# THE WEST MIDLANDS

Compiled by the West Midlands Federation
of Women's Institutes from contributions sent by
Institutes in the County

Published jointly by
Countryside Books, Newbury
and the WMFWI, Birmingham

First published 1996
© West Midlands Federation of Women's Institutes 1996

COUNTRYSIDE BOOKS
3 Catherine Road
Newbury, Berkshire

ISBN 1 85306 440 8

Front cover photograph shows Mr R Powell setting
out with his daughters from Yardley.

Back cover photograph shows a tram on
the Stratford road in Sparkhill.

Produced through MRM Associates Ltd., Reading
Printed by Woolnough Bookbinding Ltd., Irthlingborough

# CONTENTS

WALSALL

WOLVERHAMPTON

DUDLEY

BIRMINGHAM

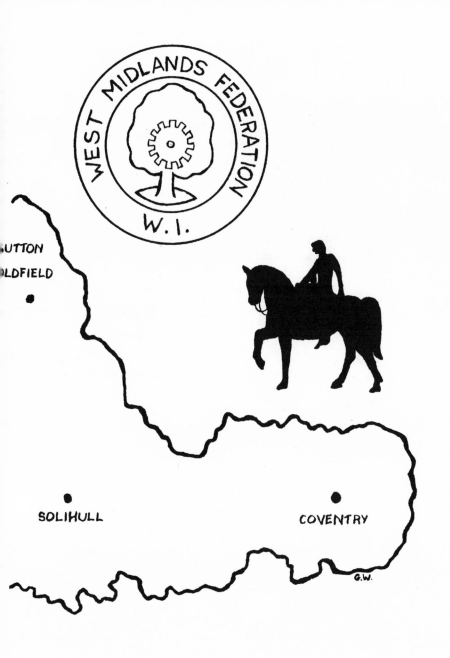

WEST MIDLANDS FEDERATION W.I.

SUTTON
COLDFIELD

SOLIHULL

COVENTRY

G.W.

# ACKNOWLEDGEMENTS

The West Midlands Federation of Women's Institutes would like to thank all the members and their friends who took time and trouble to submit articles for inclusion in this book and for the use of many photographs. For reasons of space and to prevent repetition it was not possible to include every article, but all were, without exception, of value in determining the shape of the finished book.

Thanks are also due to the many people who assisted with typing. Without the beautiful drawings prepared by Gill Wiley of Heart of England WI and Bee Turner of Berkswell WI, the pleasure in this book would be greatly diminished.

*Innes Brett*
*Co-ordinator*

# FOREWORD

This book is a valuable and historical record of a 'new county'. The West Midlands was formed following the boundary changes of 1974. With Birmingham, Britain's second city, at its heart, the West Midlands combines the best of both worlds, a great and interesting industrial past and present and some of the richest farmland to be found anywhere in the country. From the internationally known Jewellery Quarter of Birmingham to the area which Shakespeare knew and wrote of as his Forest of Arden with its villages and bluebell woods, there is much to see and appreciate both historically and within its contemporary use. The rural areas form the green lungs of the two great cities of Birmingham and Coventry.

The reminiscences within this book are the memories of people who have lived through amazing and far reaching upheaval. The vast changes brought about by two world wars, the changes in working practices in both town and country, the ease with which people now travel, at home and overseas, have all combined to change life fundamentally in this century. All these events have been faithfully recorded by WI members and their friends.

I commend this book to you as a valuable record of the past and, I hope, as a pleasurable and interesting source of information for the future.

*Innes Brett*
*County Chairman*

# TOWN & COUNTRY LIFE

# SOME TOWNS AND VILLAGES
# REMEMBERED

*Here are just a few 'snapshots' of life in our towns and villages as it used to be – lamplighters, blacksmiths, roads so quiet they were our playgounds. It was not really so long ago!*

### ❖ STECHFORD IN THE 1920s ❖

'On 17th June 1914, a very hot day, I came into the world at 3 Station Road, Lower Stechford; so called because it was at the bottom of the hill from Stechford station, the entrance in those days being on the main Station Road, with a row of railway cottages on the left and more in Northcote Road. Parkinsons Stove Company on the right-hand side was in a dip. Further on Levis made noted motorbikes in Albert Road. Houses were on either side as far as the railway bridge with high banks and then more houses going on to Stechford village.

Quite a number of pupils had to walk to school from Lea Hall; no station there at that time, and most were from the farming fraternity.

As children we ganged up, and could be heard chanting to Catholic children:

Catholic, Catholic, quack, quack, quack,
Go to the Devil and never come back.

Likewise, they had their say:

Holy Father, I've killed a cat.
Well my child, why did you do that?
Holy Father, what will it be?
Forty days without no tea.
Holy Father, that's too long.
Well my child, why did you do wrong?
Holy Father, it was a Protestant cat.
Well my child, I'll forgive you for that!

For flicking a rubber with a ruler, two of us were caught when Sir walked in. Off to the Head for a stroke of the cane. Not me – let's go to the loo instead. Pity the classroom door opened, and "he" saw us coming the wrong way. So it was two strokes for me!

Time came when we were old enough to go to housewifery held in Acocks Green. It was like going abroad to go that far on a bus. Two teachers lived in the large house. We learnt to wash, starch and iron. Beds were made, floors, grates, windows etc were cleaned, but what good grounding it was.

Houses were being built in large numbers towards Hobmoor Lane, and the Bordesley Green area. News came that older pupils were being transferred to a new school in Bierton Road, now demolished I believe. What a venture from a village school to a large modern one, meeting children from all walks of life. One day we were walking along a corridor on our way to PE in the playground. Serge gymslips, white blouses, yellow and navy ties, thick black stockings, plus red, green or blue bands for whichever team we represented. My attention was drawn to the boys in a classroom. Suddenly someone shouted – too late. I had fallen down a manhole. It so happened a man was working there, back bent, and I landed on him. I was a bonny lass and had several nicknames, one being "Two and a half", but the rumours that went round school about him being injured, and taken to hospital were not true.

It is so hard to imagine fields all round the Stechford area, going right through to Yardley, with Kents Moat, Chelmsley Woods into Marston Green; Spion Cop where the baths are now built; sheep and cows being driven down Flaxley Lane to the butcher's opposite our house. One day several of us watched through a crack when a pig was killed. Then there was Drakeleys Fair over the river; and Mother having to push my sister and me to Erdington to visit relatives.

Back to Higher Stechford, trailing up the hill to Sunday school (Baptist) held in the lovely Masonic Hall on the corner of Station Road and Manor Road. At Mr Edginton's store we were allowed behind the counter. Soldiers were around, mainly on crutches, George and Charlie being two favourites.

Later on shops were built by Ford the builder who had a large house in Old Lode Lane. There were comments that they would not last long. They have.

We were allowed to participate in concerts held at the Wesleyan Methodist church, since demolished. How we enjoyed performing *Caller Herring* dressed as fisher girls singing "Who'll buy my Caller Herring?" The new Baptist chapel was built further along Victoria Road. My father was a deacon; he was also asked as a carpenter and joiner to make the reading desk and other things required in the chapel.

Continuing over Albert Road and into Morden Road, we used to visit Morden Park where we paddled in the river Cole. Someone was very ill at one time in Albert Road and a sort of peat was put over the road to deaden the noise of horse and cart traffic.

In that vicinity too lived the Miss Neweys. The family had a small factory in Birmingham making hooks and eyes and press studs.

Several times a year men arrived by train to attend the races at Bromford. In orderly fashion they proceeded down the hill, past "our shop" to the Fox and Goose, and along Bromford Lane, usually with several policemen around.

After the 1914–18 war, work was very difficult to find for returning soldiers, although my father did manage to find something over Hams Hall way for a little while. Not a lot of people owned houses in those days, and a landlord would allow a tenant to turn their front room into a shop, so this became our new venture. Apart from repairing furniture, books, pictures, chairs etc were bought and sold. Old Mann from round the corner spent hours browsing through the books – never bought anything. The opportunity came to extend as the folk next door were leaving. This enabled "Glass cut to Order" to be transferred from the garden into the house, as upstairs and downstairs could be used. What a day when a crate arrived from the potteries, delving into the straw to bring out plates, cups, saucers and dishes, decorated chamber pots, rejects from LMS Hotels etc. Every Wednesday afternoon the shop was closed, and my parents went to the warehouse in Edgbaston Street to order pots, pans and other household goods.

Cycles and accessories came next. Carbide lamps, and with carbide the smell was awful. Then came the oil filled ones, red or white oil costing 2d a bottle, progressing to flat type batteries, and bulbs, as well as selling nails, screws, "cats whiskers", crystals, nuts and bolts etc. Folk came from near and far – if you couldn't get whatever at Inchleys, you couldn't get it anywhere. There were grumbles, especially if something cost sixpence at Woolworths.

Cycles were the next thing for sale. A Hercules cost £3 19s 9d. My aunt bought one for me, and I loved it. When I was courting BSA had just produced a double diamond tandem with de-railleur gears, and we had a lot of pleasure cycling many miles. Of course, selling cycles meant stocking tyres, spokes, inner tubes, pumps, connections and repair outfits.

Then it was time to leave school, and go to Margaret Street in Birmingham to see what work was available, at the Education Office.'

### ❊ LIFE IN COVENTRY BEFORE THE FIRST WORLD WAR ❊

'Hearing about Coventry and its up and coming future, my grandfather's family decided to try a new way of life. They left their Wiltshire inn and moved to Coventry. The children were getting to working age and it was decided to go back to inn life and they took over the Rising Sun Inn in Spon Street. Mum stayed home to help. My father was by this time also back in Coventry and found a job as a butcher's

*Stratford Road, Sparkhill when trams were the main form of public transport.*

assistant. He delivered meat to the Rising Sun, and met Mum. He secretly courted her and they decided to have their picture taken together. It was displayed in the photographer's window. My grandfather, taking a stroll one day, saw it. Poor Mum – his anger was terrifying. She was sent off to London and became mother's help to a young newly-married daughter of a Coventry businessman with whom she became great friends. The two of them had jaunts to Drury Lane Theatre, the Crystal Palace, the parks. However, Dad, not daunted, visited London and the courtship continued. By this time he was working for Rudge-Whitworth, having developed a keen engineering sense. He became a pioneer cyclist, winning trophies at The Butts Stadium, riding in the Godiva Processions, etc. They became engaged and married in 1907. Around the time of my birth he rode with a team of Rudge-Whitworth men from Land's End to John o' Groats in record time for which he was given a medal.

Motor-cycles at this time came on the scene. Dad found his niche. He became inventive and launched many improvements. His ambition was to start his own engineering business. My brother was born in 1910 and my sister in 1912. Mum was like a hen with chicks. Very protective. I was not sent to school until I was turned six when I was "found" by the School Board man. "Be good sweet maiden, let those who will, be clever", came to Mum before the three Rs! By this time we lived next door to one of her sisters and I went to school with my cousin. We caught measles and passed it on to the smaller children. My brother developed pneumonia and a little girl cousin meningitis. They died within hours of each other, at Eastertime. To this day the strong perfume of narcissus, flowers in the many wreaths, makes me feel very sad. There was a double funeral. My elder cousin and I wore black and white check frocks for mourning. I wore a very plain leghorn straw hat with a black band. Never in my life since do I remember the envy I felt when I saw my cousin's beautiful white silk-straw confection of a bonnet tied with white satin ribbons! Mum was demented with grief. Her obsession was to visit London Road cemetery, to where we regularly traipsed with my aunt and her children, carrying bunches of wilting flowers. I hated the atmosphere of the cemetery, the awful sadness and the, to me, menacing weirdly shaped trees.

In 1914 the war came. Dad was exempt because of his skill in engineering. A munitions factory was built, White and Poppe, and he was employed there. A colony of small breeze-block bungalows was erected to house the employees, people from all walks of life. Doctors, technicians, nurses, skilled workmen, labourers and young women came from all over Britain anxious to take advantage of high wages in the dangerous production of gunpowder. Their work turned their skins a bright yellow and they were called "Tetrol girls". They wore blue overalls and mob-caps.

Our doctor said that Mum must get away from where we lived and in desperation Dad decided to move to one of "the huts" as they were dubbed. Too far away to walk to the cemetery. We moved during a bitterly cold January. We had lived in a circumspect area of criss-cross streets, a long way from fields or a park. Our new home consisted of a large living room, two bedrooms and a fair sized kitchen. We had electric lights. No more sickly hissing gaslight and fiddly gas mantles. No more mid-house cold, dark stairs. My sister and I could just cross the room into our bedroom, leaving the door slightly ajar so that we could hear the murmur of our parents' talk and see reflections on the wall from the large black range, bliss! In the summer we could, with Mum, walk a few yards and over a railway bridge into fields. We had picnics with our dolls, Mum with her sewing, eating cos lettuce sandwiches, home-made rock cakes and cold tea in a bottle. We loved it! Running to the railway fence to watch and wonder where the trains were going.

School was a problem. With so many newcomers to the district there were no vacancies. Mum heard of a small private school run by a mother and daughter. These so-called dame schools were quite common in those days. I was sent there – half a crown a week. The least said the better about my education, though I did make lifelong friends. My sister, too, came when she was five, but luckily a new school was built which she then attended. Too late for me, I was getting on for leaving time. In spite of wearying queues for food, the fear of Zeppelin raids, the anxiety for uncles fighting in France (Mum's youngest brother was killed in his nineteenth year), they were busy happy times. The family eked out rations to send parcels to France. The children crayoned funny pictures, and wrote letters to send.

"Home on leave" were red letter days of jollification. Mum made chocolate from something called "cocoa-butter" and a sticky toffee from a precious tin of condensed milk.

When war ended the munitions factory closed. Our wartime friends went back to their original homes. Dad, more determined than ever to become his own boss, concentrated on this, and moving into a proper house took second place. He found a small factory premises, partners. Had a stand at the motor-cycle show at Olympia to promote his ideas and inventions. I remember the never-ending patent fees to be met at Somerset House. . .alas, it was wrong timing during the after-war slump. The verge of bankruptcy. Nightmarish!'

## ◼ COVENTRY BETWEEN THE WARS ◼

'I was born in Coventry in the mid 1920s. We lived near the city centre, not all that far from the original city walls, in a house built in the late 1890s city expansion. My parents both came from first generation ex-country stock, my father having been moved to Coventry by his company. He was an insurance inspector. His job gave us certain privileges. It was a steady, though not well paid one, but he was allowed a small company car and, as the office was a bedroom at home, a telephone, both of which we were allowed to use as long as strict checks were kept on mileage and phone calls paid for.

Coventry was, at that time, still a small market town. The centre was full of quaint narrow streets full of timber-framed buildings and the whole was dominated by the two big medieval churches, St Michael's, the cathedral, and Holy Trinity. We attended the former, where I was both christened and confirmed and my father was a cathedral chorister, voluntary of course, for many years. Indeed, the last time I was in the cathedral was for my confirmation service in April 1940, wearing the conventional white dress. By then, however, we had moved out to Green Lane, an estate built in the early 1930s, about two miles out and within an easy walk of the country.

Coventry was still very small, I remember clearly to my cost. As a small child, I never went "up the town" (it was literally nearly all uphill), with either of my parents, but that they met many people they knew and I was kept, an unwilling listener, while they chatted. You could go to most places by tram, the station up the Albany Road to visit my godmother, Broadgate, even to Bedworth. My sister, eight years my senior and a pupil at Barr's Hill school, got her bike wheels caught in the tram lines coming down Bishop Street hill, had a nasty fall, and declared she'd never ride a bike again. All of which resulted in me never learning to ride a bike! My father also had a nasty experience with a tram, this time at the bottom of Bishop Street Hill. A tram slid backwards down the hill, my father's car was trapped at the bottom. The tram landed up being stopped by the car's bumper bar. It says much for the workmanship of our old Jowett two-seater that the front of the car wasn't even dented!

Going on a trip on a wet day in the Jowett was uncomfortable. The canvas hood was put up. Mary sat in the dicky seat with an umbrella to keep off the worst of the weather. I had to sit inside between Mother and Father. This meant I was astride the gear lever and got bashed every time Father changed gear. In fine weather it was much more comfortable. I was allowed to travel in the dicky seat as long as Mary held firmly on to my coat!

We stood at the bottom of our road, Regent Street, and watched the Godiva Procession go past when Miss Muriel Mellerup was acting as Godiva. She rode her own white horse and much of her hair was her own, she could sit on it, and the whole thing was very dignified and impressive. I also stood and watched the animals from the Bertram Mills Circus going from the station up to Hearsall Common for the performances. Tuesday was "cow day". The abbatoir was in the next street, York Street. The poor creatures were brought into the city by train and driven on foot down Queen's Road – my route to and from school. Very frequently the drovers were drunk and used to run the animals, who were terrified. I used to slip inside people's garden gates – a little bit like playing musical chairs – to let a herd go by. I hated Tuesdays!

My mother belonged to the cathedral Mothers' Union. I was too young to understand the system, but she seemed to have a certain number of old ladies allocated to her to visit, I presume to make sure that they were all right. These ladies lived in the courts in Much and Little Park Streets, and in school holidays I loved going with Mother on these visits. We went down an alley between two very old houses and came out into a rectangular courtyard, paved with grey bricks with diamond-shaped patterns on them, and surrounded by small red brick houses. A pump stood in the centre of the yard.

On looking back, I think these little cottages must have been one room up, one room down, for the room we went into contained a blackleaded range with an oven beside it and, usually under the window, a high, brown coloured stone sink. No sign of stairs – they must have been behind a door in the wall and no sign of a loo anywhere, inside or out. The window was small and always had a half net curtain – spotlessly clean – and a row of geranium pots on the window sill, keeping out most of the light. Yes, slums they might have been, but they were beautifully clean, as indeed were the old ladies themselves. They usually wore dark clothing and always, as I remember, a spotless wrap-over sleeveless pinafore in flowered cotton. But the real attraction for me as a child were the cats. I was dotty over cats, even in those days. Always there was a large well-fed cat – black, tabby or ginger – well cared for and obviously much loved. In summer I sat on the doorstep, the house only seemed to have one door to the outside, in winter I sat on a stool near the range. And I nursed the cat. I didn't care how long Mother chatted, I was happy!'

## ▨ THE PELSALL POLICEMAN ▨

'In the 1920s our village policeman was Mr Rushton, to be seen daily riding his bicycle with his cape folded over the handlebars. Any child seen doing "what he hadn't oughta" got a swipe with that cape and a stern warning. Very efficient.

Years before it had been a fineable offence to set fire to a chimney to clear the soot. If you couldn't afford a sweep you watched for the policeman to go to Rushall on Friday to collect his wages. When he returned there was a pall of smoke over the village but he couldn't pinpoint the offending chimneys.'

## ▨ DOWN TO THE BULL RING MARKET ▨

'The Bull Ring market in the years before the war was a wonderfully exciting place. Open stalls all down the hill vied with each other for custom, as the vendors shouted their wares. At dusk on winter afternoons, they lit their oil lamps and continued plying their trade in the flickering yellow glare. All manner of marvellous goods were on sale, from fruit and vegetables to fish, crockery to clothing, second-hand tools to sweeties. Anything, in fact, that could be transported there on a handcart, could be found in that noisy, smelly place. There too, was the lady with her "'Andy carriers", the match-sellers, and dotted periodically down the hill, the small army of beggars. Some had little trays, others just held out a cap to passers-by. Some were ex-servicemen with only one arm or one leg, or were blind. Some had notices: "Wife and children to support", or "Homeless and jobless". Normally they tugged my heartstrings, but on this particular Saturday nothing could make me sad. For we were on our way to the Market Hall to buy me a dog.

For years Mother had held out. No pets of any kind. But with a music exam looming, she rashly promised that if I did well, she might reconsider. To everyone's astonishment, including my own, I achieved marks of 95% so she had no option but to honour her vow. Through the jostling crowds we made our way, fat ladies with men's cloth caps on their heads and quite a few barefoot children amongst the throng, into the Market Hall itself. Up to the pet stall we bowled, there to study the livestock. Quite a variety met the eye. Day-old chicks, peeping in their tiny boxes, sleepy kittens curling together for warmth and several sorts of dog. As soon as I saw "Pat" (for that was the name I had pre-chosen) I knew she was the one I wanted. "That one, Mum," I whispered, "can I have that one?" "What kind is it?" she asked the stallholder, and was told, "A cross-collie ma'am, lovely little dog."

"Hmm," pondered Mother. "Will it grow big, I can't abide big dogs?" The man assured her that the puppy would only achieve medium size. Then Mother had misgivings about having a bitch, the significance of which of course was beyond me. "No trouble, Missus," the man assured her and my eyes implored. Finally after much consideration agreement was reached. For the sum of 7s 6d the little furry creature was mine. Few moments in my life have equalled the one when the warm wriggling little body was put into my arms. With a heart bursting with happiness, I carried her back through the throngs, onto the tram and bore her home.'

21

'I was born in a house in Kings Heath – one of three in Valentine Road built by my grandfather's firm for his younger son, my father, and his two married daughters. His unmarried daughter lived with him and was secretary of the family firm. She had inherited my grandfather's business acumen and it was a great loss when she died of meningitis after influenza in 1941. When I was born, my mother had a live-in nurse: the family doctor came from Hall Green and continued to come even after the introduction of the National Health Service, although we were not in his catchment area.

Kings Heath was part of the urban sprawl which developed after the Great War but it was still referred to as "The Village". It lies on the Alcester Road (A435) which is one of the arterial roads out of Birmingham. There was a library, a swimming bath where one could swim for an hour for threepence, and a police station with stables. Kings Heath railway station was in use until 1936 and had sidings serving the yards of local coal merchants. Horses were still used quite a lot: apart from the police riding their horses, the milkman and the Corona delivery man used horse-drawn carts. We always had a lump of sugar ready to feed the horses.

*An early road accident in Birmingham in 1907.*

There was the Kingsway cinema, independent of the big organisations. The manager was an important person in the area and wore a dinner jacket when *Gone with the Wind* was being shown. I saw *Snow White and the Seven Dwarfs* and other famous films there and, more particularly, the Pathé News. I remember the first pictures of Belsen and the concentration camps and, earlier in the war, selected newsreels of the fighting. I also remember the first pictures of the devastation of Hiroshima and Nagasaki and the shadow of a man negatived on a wall. The cinema was our education as well as our entertainment.

There are two parks, Kings Heath and Uffculme. The latter was bequeathed by the Chamberlain family. The parks were part of Highbury, the house where Joseph Chamberlain lived; it was a nursing home during the war and is now a conference centre for Birmingham City Council. I remember being taken to feed the ducks in the park and to see the shire horses which pulled the gang mowers. When we were older, we played in the park on our own, supervised by parkkeepers in uniform who kept us all in order. Round the park had been iron railings which were taken during the war for munitions. Kings Heath park housed the Birmingham Horticultural School.

The butcher on the corner of High Street and Poplar Road had his own abbatoir on the premises and, occasionally, cows were herded along Valentine Road. One ran into our front garden, doing a great deal of damage.'


🔲  WIND AND SNOW  🔲

'When I was a teenager my friends and I would quite often decide to walk to Marston Green and "The Bluebell Woods" at Chelmsley Woods. On this particular Sunday, 14th June 1931, only two of us went, myself and friend Hilda. It was a good walk over seven fields and it was our custom to come back on the train, it only cost a few coppers. I remember sitting on a bench at the station and looking towards Birmingham. The sky was as black as pitch. You can imagine our consternation when we left the train and reached the main road to find scenes of great devastation – shop windows blown out, hoardings ripped down, trees and debris littered the road. We found out afterwards that it had been caused by a tornado which had swept across Small Heath towards Tyseley. Immense damage had occurred at Small Heath Park and a well known grocery shop – Fraziers on the Coventry Road – was completely destroyed. Miraculously there was only one fatality, a woman who lived in Formans Road, Sparkhill. The family were very glad to see me get back home safe and sound.'

'The winter of 1947 was severe, with heavy snowfalls followed by freezing winds. It caused chaos everywhere. Fuel stocks were very low and the advent of that winter was a further toll on a country already stretched to the limit after the war.

At Solihull the roads were banked on either side with frozen snow, upon which children loved to play games of Kings and Castles. The grown ups just shovelled and cursed the weather. The roads themselves were inches thick with pack-ice as the low volume of traffic just could not disperse it. Numbers of German ex-prisoners of war, awaiting repatriation, were set to work clearing the High Street. It was so cold and most of them were very young, so shopkeepers would take hot drinks out to them in sympathy. Somehow they had ceased to be "the enemy", hated just a short time ago.

The Midland Red buses served us as best they could in the conditions. City buses didn't come further than the boundary in Olton. Most of us walked some of the way, being picked up by the bus when it finally came along. There was so much humour, and so many friends made that winter.'

## ◈ GOING 'UP ERDINGTON' ◈

'One of the regular treats of my childhood in the 1920s was when my parents decided to take us children "up Erdington" on a Saturday afternoon. It was most pleasant in the autumn and winter when, after the shopping was done, we came home in the twilight having purchased some pikelets to toast by the bright coal fire.

By the time we arrived home the lamplighter would have been round, turning on the gas-lit street lamps.'

'Born in 1910, I was first taken to Minworth in a pram with my parents and brothers and sister, and as I grew up spent so much time there, weekends and holidays. My grandfather lived in the house that was "The Websters" of the Iron Men of Penns fame where wire was first made in the Midlands (before the reservoirs were made). My grandfather was in charge of the pump house, which was kept in a shiny and spotless condition. It was controlled by the Water Department at the Council House and the horses that were then used for the Corporation were brought there for resting and shoeing. I remember being allowed to blow the bellows on the furnace many times in the forge. There used to be a water wheel by the waterfall, but it deteriorated and was dismantled when I was quite small.

The employees at the Council House were allowed to fish there. Grandma made them lovely teas, and I used to help take the food to them.

We used to help ourselves to the apples in the orchard, stuff them up our jumpers, and go to the canal and throw them to the bargees,

*Alcester Road, Moseley in quieter days early in the century.*

as we thought they were poor and hungry (goodness help us if Grandad caught us).

I learned to swim and skate there. My father was a good skater and made all us children skates out of old files and screwed them on to our boots. My uncles used to take us on the lake in the two punts kept in the punt house, the remains of which are still there. There were lots of swallows' nests in this and it was lovely to see them skimming the water. There were also kingfishers by the smaller lakes.

The wild flowers were lovely. We would pick them, and Grandma would name them for us. One of my uncles made us whistles out of cow parsley stems.

Col Baker, co-director of Kersons, bought the area just before the war hoping to make a bird sanctuary out of it, but tragically he was killed in the war. It lay uncared for for a long time, then Rawling Bros took it over and started filling in the lakes. They were going to use the whole area for dumping rubbish, but happily were stopped in the throes.'

## ▨ EASTERN GREEN ▨

'My early childhood was spent in Eastern Green; we lived in Corner Cottage on the corner of Eastern Green Lane and Pickford Green Lane. In those days it stood well out in the country, not in Coventry city suburbs as it does now.

The church and village school were the centre of local activities together with the parish room, which was an ex-army hut erected by local men and used for social gatherings including whist drives and dances. The school itself had many pupils from surrounding districts. Children walked to attend from Back Lane, Four Oaks and Harvest Hill, distances of over two miles, hurrying when they heard the single school bell being rung – lateness was punished.

The annual event in the village was the church fete held on the vicarage lawn. Adjoining the lawn was a large pond and the local kids really enjoyed a boating trip on a punt propelled by a Mr T. Sammons (he owned the woodyard and sawmill at Harvest Hill).

Next door to our cottage were workshops belonging to a local tradesman, Mr Holmes. He was a carpenter and wheelwright and made ladders and carts. As a secondary trade he was also the village undertaker and he made coffins in his sheds. Many a local was conveyed to the churchyard on one of his carts.

One of the sheds facing Pickford Green Lane was the village blacksmith's. A visiting smith used to attend to shoe local farm horses. As kids, our delight was to help pump the bellows prior to the shoes being fitted – what a smell of burning hoof!

Travel was very limited. One day a week the "Bunty" bus went to and from the city, but most people depended on local door to door deliveries. I remember the Co-op grocery van, and the "oil man" who delivered paraffin for lighting – there was no electricity in the village at this time. One man from the Barracks market used to call about once a month selling ladies' hats. He drove a motor bike fitted with a large box sidecar full of hats in cardboard boxes.

In those days traffic was more or less non-existent in Eastern Green, but we had to make sure front gates were shut when sheep or cattle were being driven to market or moved from field to field – an open gate and in they would come!'

---

# CHURCH AND CHAPEL

*At the heart of the community was the church or chapel. Many families observed Sunday as a strict day of rest, and most children attended Sunday school – in fact, it provided them with a much loved treat and outing once a year.*

### ▣ SUNDAY SCHOOL AT LONGFORD ▣

'My mother's family had been staunch Baptists for several generations and attended Salem Baptist church at Longford, a village to the north of Coventry. The fields at the back of the churchyard are still called the Meeting Fields as the very first services were held there before a chapel was constructed in 1765. It was during the lifetime of this building that my grandmother, as a young woman, decided to become a member and was duly baptised in the canal by Longford bridge.

By the time I was ready to start Sunday school in 1930, a very imposing building had evolved from the old chapel, including a sunken tank with steps either side, which was filled with water for the baptisms. The candidates dressed in white, the minister stood in the tank with the water waist high, and each young man or woman was totally immersed. However, to Sunday school. At first we met in the large schoolroom which was underneath the chapel, but another building was planned, to be called the New School. Members were invited to donate five shillings to have their initials engraved on a brick. The new building was a great success, having a large lobby, a room downstairs for the juniors and one upstairs for the seniors, and it was here that the basis of my religious instruction was founded.

The chapel also provided a fair amount of our social lives. There were garden parties, concerts and Sunday school outings, and a great event, the Treat, which was held on Whit Monday, when bank holidays really were bank holidays. All the Sunday schools in the area would assemble with their banners. These were large and colourful, similar to the banners of the trade unions. A procession would then take place, each contingent following, some on foot and some on gaily decorated floats. We always felt rather privileged, as we were led by our Scout group's drum and fife band. After the procession we dispersed, each Sunday school going to its own local field to continue the festivities. As we passed through the gate, we were each given a bun and an orange and on one occasion in 1930, we received a medal to commemorate Robert Raikes, who had founded Sunday schools 150 years earlier in 1780. I still have the medal today. The afternoon was filled with games and races, and sturdy swings were fixed up in the trees on the edge of the field. We also partook of a bumper tea which was set out on long trestle tables. I just loved the seed cake which was always there in abundance, although it seemed most unpopular with others.

Another important event, though of a more serious nature, was the Sermons. This was actually the Sunday school Anniversary, and was held in April, but no one ever called it other than the Sermons. How this originated I really don't know, but I thought it sounded much more grand. For weeks beforehand the choirmaster would train us to sing special songs and hymns and the excitement grew to fever pitch as the day drew near. Everyone had new clothes, the girls a riot of colour in dresses and, of course, straw hats. I remember one year in particular when my hat was ruched under the brim with pink silk and sported a bunch of cherries at the side. I felt very pleased with myself as there was always a bit of rivalry between the girls which had nothing to do with the true spirit of the occasion.

There were two services, one on the Sunday afternoon and one in the evening. People visited from all around the neighbourhood and were packed in like sardines, extra seats being placed in the aisles and every available corner. We children of course had our places in the gallery along with the adult choir, and right in the centre was the orchestra which was composed of local men. I can feel the thrill now as the conductor tapped his stick to commence the Introit, and we just let rip. We always had visiting ministers for these services and did our best to impress them. During the next few weeks, other chapels held their Sermons, and we would visit them. They really were the highlight of our Sunday school year.'

## ◼ CHAPEL EVENTS ◼

'A day out in a charabanc with the Sunday school was the only chance many children had of getting away from Pelsall in the 1920s. We had two chapels, Primitive Methodist and Wesleyan, and the diehards of the one would not dream of crossing the doorstep of the other. The parish church seemed very remote in my early days. Chapel events most enjoyed by us children were Sunday school Anniversaries and Harvest Festivals. The dress for these occasions was uncompromising. Girls in white – no colours at all – and boys in grey shorts and white shirts with a blue striped tie. Early May could be quite cold so I was made to wear the usual winter underwear of combinations, liberty bodice, navy fleece-lined knickers, and long black stockings with garters.'

*Birmingham's Cambridge Road Methodist church Anniversary, always a special day in the year.*

## ◼ NEVER ON SUNDAY ◼

'We always wore "Sunday clothes", complete with hat, for church. These clothes were eventually relegated to ordinary wear when new Sunday outfits were bought. Grandad never worked on Sunday, not even in the garden, and we were not allowed to play cards or sew. "God provides Sunday for rest and praise" was his saying, but finally his influence wore off and we became very relaxed about our Sundays.'

## ◼ KEEPING THE CHAPEL GOING ◼

'Both my parents were Methodist and there was a small chapel in Meriden. When my father, with his mother and three unmarried sisters, came to Warwickshire from Cheshire in 1892, they attended this little church, and so my mother attended when she married and became very involved. My father took Sunday school until someone came to help. Mother organised a concert sometimes. How she managed I don't know as she had a family and had to come two miles in horse and trap. If we had no organist she would play the organ and I have heard her say that she had played with a baby on her knee.

When we were small we went to a house nearby run by a C of E lady for afternoon Sunday school. We all went to service at eleven o'clock and Father went alone at night. At night we had hymns and prayers by Mother but she encouraged us to take part. We always had a fire in the dining room on Sundays and we entertained the preachers. A cab brought three men from Coventry, one for Fillongley, one for Meriden and one for Balsall Common and fetched them back after evening service. We had many notable Methodist ministers stay with us. When my sisters were old enough they took Sunday school and my cousin ran a young womens' class. They also played the organ.'

## ◼ INCREASING THE CONGREGATION ◼

'Sunday school and evening service were a must in my family, always sitting in the same seats. One parson formed a football club with the proviso that each member must attend evening service every Sunday. Consequently the back seats in the church were filled with young men who had probably never seen the inside of a church before.'

### ▣ Our Chapel ▣

'Our local church at Earlswood was a small Methodist chapel in a field on its own within a short walking distance of the farm. We all went there to Sunday school which was then at 3 pm, and then as we got older to the church service at 6.30 pm. There was a tin hut at the back of the brick built church and two privies across the field. Also a lean-to kitchen at the side of the hut, again of corrugated iron with a brick floor, a hand pump for the water and an enamel bowl for washing up. It was dark and damp and inconvenient.

The tin hut had a corner stove which was fired by coke with a chimney going up through the roof. This used to get red hot. Most dangerous but no one ever got burned. We would gather round it for stories, colouring or plasticine modelling. The plasticine was always hard and a murky brown colour after much pummelling and reuse. You could not go out and buy anything new so it was saved from week to week in water and softened on the stove before we used it. Miss Horten played the piano for us and as a special treat we'd be allowed to march round whilst singing "Praise Him, praise Him, all ye little children". I remember sitting on the seed drill while Mary, the land girl, walked behind as I sang "Jesus bids us shine" to her. I could not comprehend that she did not know it and had never been to Sunday school. It was all so much part of our lives with "the party" being the highlight of the year with bread, marg, jelly and a bun each for tea. We learned many lessons there, often not appreciating it at the time.

It was not enjoyed by everyone, especially the Anniversary Sunday. This was great for the extroverts as they sang or recited a psalm wearing their best clothes but for those that were shy it was just a pain and embarrassment. One year my youngest brother became bored and visited the toilet so many times he was nicknamed "commercial traveller". It was not worth stopping him just in case it was genuine need that made him go out. We practised for this one night a week for some time beforehand. No one would go to the practice until *Dick Barton Special Agent* had been listened to on the radio before starting out on foot or bicycle.

One lesson I remember was of a conscientious carpenter who polished a table underneath as well as on top. When he was asked, "Why bother as no one can see the underside?" he replied, "But God can." We would complain when the preachers were dry and boring and especially about one little old man whose false teeth almost dropped out as he talked although this did cause some amusement. I think now how unkind we were. But a much loved elderly teacher called Mrs Wiseman, and very like her name she was, would chide us and say, "Just remember they are doing their best."'

## ▧ A DIFFERENT DAY ▧

'I remember each Sunday in the 1920s being the same, so very different from every other day in the week. Breakfast consisted of faggots fetched the day before from a shop in Silver Street, Coventry, in an enamel can.

We wore our best clothes, including button boots in the winter. By ten o'clock we were at the Wesleyan Methodist Sunday school in Lockhurst Lane, Foleshill. As a small child I sat on a primary chair, and later on a bench. Girls sat on one side of the Sunday school, boys on the other.

At eleven o'clock we joined our parents, relatives and friends in the chapel. I sat in the gallery with the choir, next to my auntie. During the sermon I used to draw pictures of the hats worn by the ladies.

With my auntie and cousin I then walked to a cemetery, to put flowers on our ancestors' graves. With us we took a crippled uncle, whom we pushed in a basket wheelchair.

Dinner was always Yorkshire pudding with gravy, eaten first. Then a roast and a pudding. Grandma's house was a little cottage, and the washing up was done on a tin tray on the kitchen table, the hot water poured into a bowl from a kettle on the blackleaded range.

At 2.30 we went to Sunday school again. This time we joined classes, read from the Bible and had text cards. When we collected ten small ones we had one large one to hang in our bedrooms. Sunday tea was special; sometimes having tinned salmon, tinned fruit and cream and fancy cakes. This we shared with relatives and friends.

Once again we walked to chapel for the evening service. It was early bed, but sometimes I sat up for supper, when we had cold meat and we sang around the piano, which my brother played.

A special Sunday was one when it was the Anniversary, usually called the Sermons, for there was a visiting preacher who took three services, a sermon at each. Special hymns were sung, which we had practised for many weeks beforehand, and it was an honour if you were chosen to sing a solo – standing on a stool, in the raised pulpit. All the girls had new dresses, the colour of which one kept secret from one's friends. Bedworth Pink was a favourite colour, and the material was a shiny satin. The chapel was always full with chairs down the aisles, and in hot weather all the doors were kept open. On this Sunday my Grandma opened her front door – the only time in the year that we didn't have to go up an entry to the back door.'

---

# GETTING ABOUT

*F rom the days of the horse and cart to the motor car, from trams and cycles to the early passenger flights – what changes we have seen over the past century!*

## ▦ HORSEPOWER ▦

'Horsepower meant exactly that. The village boasted a few cars, but not many, and the largest belonged to the lady of the manor.

Each morning, her chauffeur would drive her out on her daily constitutional, always at the same time, and always by the same route. This fact was not lost upon the village children. If any little boy raised his cap on seeing her, she would stop the car and present him with some sweets.

Boys don't wear caps now, and would probably not know to raise them to adults if they did. But I doubt if their more sophisticated pleasures could equal our enjoyment in riding home on top of the last cartload, after a day in the harvest field, or of watching the carter drive his heavy draught horse across the ford over the river, especially when the water was running high.

The huge horse would emerge on the other side streaming and blowing, and the carter would lift us up onto the tailboard and carry us back to the village with our hands full of primroses and cowslips, gathered from the railway banks.

Our mother would accept her flowers, and resignedly light a fire under the kitchen copper to bathe away the river mud from us and our clothes, and oh, the bliss when the square iron door of the copper was swung wide and we were allowed to stand in the warmth of the glowing coals while we were towelled dry.

The ford has gone now, as has the horse, replaced soon after the war by a lorry which could take the longer way round to the village in half the time, and there is no traffic now beyond the bridge, built to carry only pack horses.'


## ▣ Horses and Cars ▣

'I remember a very high trap to go out visiting. Later we had a much lower one with soled rubber tyres and it was much posher, the seats were back to back and we had a very large umbrella which we called the "trap umbrella". If we went out for the day and came home late we had rugs laid in the bottom so that we could lie down and go to sleep. The back was fastened up so that we should not fall out. We used the trap to go to chapel in Meriden each Sunday. We left it at the blacksmith's shop while we were at service.

My father loved horses. We had two foals each year, one from a heavy horse and the other from a trap horse. Father broke the young

*An early car in Coventry.*

horses in himself. During the First World War the military took two
of our best horses for combat. It was a sad day. I would only be seven
but I can remember seeing them go up the drive.

If horses have never seen a donkey they are very frightened of
them. The last trap horse we had was a beautiful chestnut high step-
per. There was smoke-emitting transport on the road and this horse
was frightened of it so Father used to take the lanes when possible
after it was broken in to the shafts. One day a donkey was tethered
on the grass verge and the horse would not go by so Father got out
and led him by very slowly. The next day was market day when we
always went to Coventry for the week's provisions. Father again took
to the lanes but the horse started to drag its back legs. To cut a long
story short the vet said he was paralysed with fright. After about six
months he was no better so we had to have him put down. Father was
very sad as he loved driving a horse.

After this we bought our first car. It was not a success. It was
always breaking down. We were let down by the man from whom we
bought it. It was a Hillman. It had gate-change gears, a brass horn and
carbide brass lamps and a canvas hood. You could have put the whole

"16 kids" in a bassinet into the back. My uncle had a Hufsmobile. It was very highly sprung and when getting in, standing on the step, the other side nearly met you. We called our car Aunty Hillie and the other Uncle Huffie.

We once went to Llandudno in these two cars. Ours, the Hillman, had a radiator leak and we called at friends for a jug so that we could fill up when we saw a brook. It was very difficult to change gear when going uphill and the brakes did not hold well so Father backed to the kerb and started off again in bottom gear. Fancy starting on a journey today in a car like that. Father never bought another secondhand car.

We all went to a little village school at Eastern Green until about eleven and then went in to a Coventry school on bicycles. There were no buses until I went to Coventry and then every one and a half hours, which was the time it took to go from Birmingham to Coventry. We all knew all the drivers and conductors by name. If we were not quite ready someone would go out and ask them to wait and they would oblige.'

## ▨ WATCHING AND LISTENING ON THE ROAD ▨

'When I was a child early in the century we had to make our own entertainment, but we enjoyed watching the various things passing along the main road. Monday mornings, during holidays, were exciting, for my brother and I would wait at the end of the lane to see the cattle being driven to the cattle market at Hampton-in-Arden, except the bull, who rode in the bull float. This would be between 8 am and 10 am, then later in the day we would be at our posts again to see some animals being taken back to the various farms. Great excitement.

There lived a little way up the Kenilworth Road, a man who made the coffins for those who died in Meriden workhouse. If we saw him coming, then we had to take up our posts at the end of the lane to see if he had a coffin in the open trap. It was never covered over and jutted out from under the seat – a very rough and crude box. We had learnt a saying which went like this: "Rattle his bones over the stones, He's only a poor beggar, who nobody owns." I understand these poor old people, who sought a night's lodging in the workhouse, had to break into small pieces a heap of stones before leaving – these stones were used to mend the roads. We often had men begging for a crust of bread and Mother always gave them a lump of cheese to go with it.

We were also on the look out for the fever van – a horse-drawn affair. The driver sat in the front of the van, which was like a covered carriage but had frosted glass sides, and inside usually would be the patient suffering from either diphtheria or scarlet fever, and on their way to the fever hospital at Catherine-de-Barnes.

We all walked to church on Sunday evenings – Father in his Sunday suit and Mother in her best hat. It was all right going but coming home seemed a long way, as indeed it was. One Sunday evening during the service a man rushed into church and up to the rector and told him a Zeppelin had been seen over Coventry – the news arrived at the Bear Inn, which was the only place that had a telephone at that time. The service was brought to an abrupt end and the oil lamps extinguished immediately – I can remember being terribly frightened.

Another thing we always were listening for was the death bell. If the wind was in the right direction we could hear the church bells. During the week, if we heard three tolls and then a pause, we knew a man had died, if two tolls and a pause, it was a woman, and one for a child. We rushed into the house to tell Mother, who would immediately come outside to confirm our news.

The local doctor came from Meriden. He drove a horse and trap, quite a smart affair. We seldom had a doctor, because the cost was too much. Mother gave us brimstone and treacle on a Friday night to "clear us out", cod liver oil for sore throats, and camphor oil to rub on our chests for coughs, hot onions in our ears for earache, mustard plaster for toothache and eucalyptus oil on our handkerchiefs for colds – and a hot brick taken out of the oven for a bed-warmer. Those were the days.'


### ◈ CYCLES IN COVENTRY ◈

'In 1947 I married a Welshman who had been transferred from the then Renold Chain Works in Manchester to their Coventry branch. I found Coventry very different from the city of Edinburgh where I had spent the previous four years. Almost everybody I met worked in a factory and cycled to work. In the morning and afternoon the streets were crammed with cyclists. Then the whole place seemed to close down and in the evening the city centre was deserted.'

### ▣ RUN TO SEE THE CARS ▣

'There was very little motor traffic in Pelsall in my childhood and we didn't have a bus service until 1926. Locally owned vehicles were few; a couple of lorries and a few cars, two of the latter chauffeur driven! You could hear individual vehicles coming from a long way away and I would run out when I heard one coming to see who was in it.'

### ▣ TRAMS AND BUSES ▣

'During the 1920s my grandfather worked for Birmingham City Transport maintaining the trams in the depot. He it was who found my father a job at a time when there was great unemployment.

*The men who maintained the Birmingham City trams in the 1920s.*

My father worked for Birmingham City Transport first as a tram conductor, later as a bus conductor, and then a driver. The job was not highly paid but it was secure and of course the uniform was provided. I can remember the uniform included a thick warm overcoat and a good mackintosh. Dad always had to go to work smartly dressed with a clean shirt and collar and tie. No doubt this caused problems in those days when washing machines and spin driers were unheard of.

My memories of the trams are of the noise they made, the shining brass handles, the feel of the polished wooden seats and the steep winding stairs up to the upper deck.

A ride on the tram was always exciting especially when we went to the Lickey Hills about seven miles outside the city. We children would race upstairs and try to sit at the end of the tram which had a circular seat open to the elements. The tram would lurch and sway along the Bristol Road – it was as good as a fairground ride to us.

When I was about nine years old Dad transferred to the buses. It was my job to carry a billycan full of scalding hot tea to meet his bus. Dad would let me ride with him to the Bundy Clock and wait with him while he and his driver drank the tea and ate the packed lunch my mother had prepared for him. He would return me and the empty billycan safely back to the bus stop near home.

Being a child of a Birmingham City Transport worker meant that I had two special highlights of the year to look forward to. In the summer we would be taken by special bus from our father's depot to the sports stadium in the suburbs. There we would meet children from other depots; we ran races and played in the grounds which seemed like the country to us city dwellers. We always had a lovely tea spread out on trestle tables covered in snowy white cloths. The afternoon finished with a circus performance after which tired and happy children piled into the various buses and were taken back to the depot.

At Christmas time we were again transported by special bus, this time to Perry Barr Depot (probably the largest one in the area). We would have a Christmas party followed by a pantomime performed by children of City Transport workers. Dad used to say the children

were selected in the summer and rehearsed for months beforehand until they were ready to give a polished performance. The evening always ended with the arrival of Father Christmas who distributed large brown paper bags containing a present, sweets and an apple and orange.'


◈ **THE WAY TO FLY!** ◈

'In the late 1930s Elmdon airport (now Birmingham International Airport) was opened by the Duchess of Kent. An Imperial Airways plane was waiting on the tarmac to take her back to London. The seats in the cabin were armchairs – standard for passengers in those days!'

'I was born in May 1922 and although times were hard with poverty rife we were more fortunate than most. My father was " on the railway" in regular employment, making a great difference between a comfortable loving childhood and a loving but poor one.

My father was a Gloucester man from a poor family, who joined the London, Midland & Scottish Railway as a boy cleaner, learning all parts of the locomotive engine whilst working. At 17, he had to move to Birmingham to train as a fireman on an engine working from Saltley locomotive depot, or "The Loco" as it was called. Birmingham was smaller then with few outlying suburbs.

My brother, though younger, was a grand companion and my champion; I was a nervous child. I can still hear the street vendors calling their wares and watching children who wore boots with steel tips on them to make them last, making sparks on the paving stones. How my brother longed to own a pair, we didn't realize we didn't qualify, "our Daddy had a regular job". That golden sentence. The "good old days" of dole queues, the children's footwear queue at school and the means test. How very lucky my brother and I were,

The Great Western Railway station at Acocks Green.

but through it all people were more caring for one another with a wonderful community spirit.

At home family life revolved around the railway. We would hear the tap, tap, tap on my parents' bedroom windowpane, made by the "railway knocker-up", a man who rode around on his bicycle with a long pole which he would knock on the window to ensure the railwayman was up in time for work, no excuses for being late in those days. Railwaymen had to reside in a designated area for the railway depot.

It was not an easy task; every signal box, junction and point had to be learned for every journey undertaken, and each part of the locomotive had to be remembered. There were oral and written examinations and lastly a practical examination when a Railway Inspector travelled on the engine footplate with you to pass you as a fully fledged driver able to take goods and passenger trains to all destinations. My father was nicknamed "Main Line Jack" because he knew all lines (roads) north to Carlisle, to London and Bristol South. He was mostly an express driver. The reason he worked so hard was that every road learned enabled him to earn a higher wage.

The railway was a hard taskmaster; trains ran all minutes around the clock and mostly on time according to my father except in heavy fog. What monsters they were that took him away, sometimes to lodge at his destination. On a long journey the crew of the locomotive had to rest before bringing another train back. Oh, the joy when he came home, the smell of the engine and coal, looking in his lodging-away bag to see if he had something for us. He always did, and told us of his travels to far places. One year King George and Queen Mary visited the Industries Fair at Castle Bromwich and my father was chosen to drive the train. New overalls, what spit and polish he laughed and said he thought the coal would be whitewashed!

There were the hard times too when my father became ill. Most footplate men suffered with stomach ulcers through irregular hours, again the price of a regular job. I can remember when the railwaymen supported the striking miners; my parents always thought of others less fortunate, my father coming from a poor home understood poverty. A group of ladies would gather in Mother's kitchen to make up

43

parcels of clothes etc for the miners' families so much in need. Supporting the miners also had a price. When the strike was over the railway allowed the men back to work only on relief jobs two or three days a week. When normal hours were resumed my father remarked we had had to support them; "We still have our work to go to, those poor men have none."

He used to drive the *Royal Scot* and the *Pines Express* on the Carlisle run. When the dreaded diesel engine came along he said with a snort, "Speed! I've brought my engine down Shap Fell at 100 miles an hour plus at times, imagine it! On coal and steam." During the war years there were dreadful journeys with lines bombed etc. Mother and I worried about him and he about us as we were home alone, my brother serving in the Navy. The years took their toll and after almost 40 years' service he had to leave his beloved railway through ill health. Even so he lived to be 91 years and would tell his great grandchildren about the trains. He often dreamt of the railway, when to be an engine driver was a position to be proud of. Those romantic steam monsters that took you and your family through good and bad times but in the end provided a sound family life for your children to look back on with nostalgia because " Daddy had a regular job on the railway".'

# HOUSE&HOME

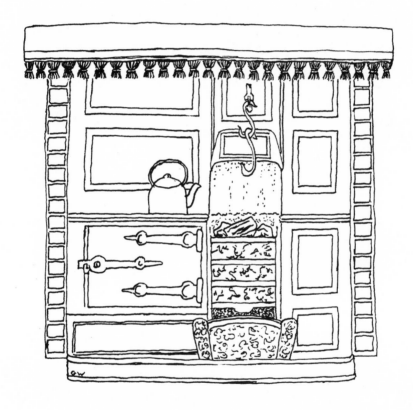

# THE WAY WE LIVED THEN

*Our way of life has changed so much in the last 50 years or so, yet even in the hardest times, there were stories of love and friendship to warm the heart.*

### ◈ CHILDHOOD IN LADYWOOD IN THE EARLY 1950s ◈

'I lived with my Mom and Dad and younger sister. We lived by a main road, in a two bedroomed house, one of which was an attic, where my sister and I shared a double bed.

We had electricity, but the gas mantles were still on the walls, somewhat the worse for wear. The one thing we did not have was running water. Instead there were two taps in the communal backyard, positioned in front of the brewhouses; these were used by eight families. There were also four toilets at the rear of the brewhouses. Two families were allocated one each. They did have wooden seats, not the sort with hinges mind you, just wooden planks with a hole cut out. They were kept immaculate, the women took it in turns to clean them. In fact they had been scrubbed that many times they were almost white.

Friday was fish and chip night, the same as most families. In those days it was a cheap meal. Or we would pop over the road, with a jug, and fetch faggots and peas. The thought makes my mouth water even now.

Mom took us to the pictures that night. My sister always had a Bounty bar to take in, and I would have a Mars bar. What a treat. We really looked forward to our night out. My sister and I would also go to the Saturday morning matinee. It was called the Regent but we called it The Bug Hole. We quite often came out with more than we went in with. The buildings were infested with all sorts of bugs, including our house. Not because we were dirty, just the oldness of the place. Mom and Dad used to fumigate the house quite often. It was called stoving. They used special sulphur candles. The bugs did

*The Brett family of Birmingham at the turn of the century.*

disappear, they went next door, until they did the same, then back they would come.

DDT powder was used on the beds. It was put on the underside, in between the springs. To catch them in the beds, my Dad would be by the bed with a bar of wet soap, my sister and I would stand by the light switch, and Mom would be standing by the side of the bed. When Dad gave the word, we switched on the light, at the same time Mom threw back the bedclothes, then Dad would slam the soap on as many bugs as he could. We were also overrun with mice, especially when the council started to demolish some of the buildings, so we always kept a cat.

The floor downstairs did not have carpets, it was lino and a couple of peg rugs, which Mom made herself. My sister and I used to help. We cut up the old coats etc into strips, then Mom pushed them through a kind of sacking with a special tool called a peg. The rug would be built up piece by piece until the sacking was covered. They lasted for years.

When it came to bathnight, which was Saturday, the peg rug would be removed from in front of the fire and a large galvanized bath would be brought in. The water was boiled in buckets on the stove. My sister and I had a bath first, always together, mind you as I started to develop I sat with my back to her. Mom had her bath when we were in bed, and Dad had his Sunday morning before anyone was up. Sometimes we went to the public baths in Monument Road. Inside were corridors with bathrooms leading off. We had to wait until one was vacant, then the woman attendant would fill the bath up for you. She had a key around her waist which turned the tap on. Before she went we had to try the water to see if it was the right temperature. During the week we had a wash in a bowl. When the water was installed it was a real luxury. The sink was fitted in an alcove in the living room, we had a curtain pulled across to hide it. My sister and I would stand in it to have a wash down.

We had a blackleaded grate. It was really economical, not only did it keep the house warm but it was used for cooking as well. On top of the fire was a hook which swung around so the kettle could be hung on it, this was nearly as black as the grate. I remember Mom used to blacklead that grate until it shone. We did our toast over the fire, quite a taste of its own, a mixture of burnt bread and smoke. We would sit on one of the boxes which we had either side of the grate. These were where the brushes and cleaning cloths were kept. Also in the hearth was a companion set, a brush, small shovel, pair of tongs and a poker, all hanging on a brass stand.

I remember many a time having to queue up outside the railway shunting yards, waiting for coal. We used to carry it in a pram. When we ran out of coal, my sister and I would go down the cellar with Dad and help him make briquettes. These were made of slack, flour and water, then they were put in small cake tins and cooked in the oven. They would keep the fire going for ages. We also went to the timber merchant and bought sticks; these were wrapped in bundles and twisted around with wire.

The chimney had to be kept clean otherwise the soot would catch fire. We kids loved it when the chimneysweep came, it was fascinating watching him, and it was our job to tell him when the brush was showing out of the chimney. It was surprising how much soot he would fetch down. This was bagged up. Soot and ashes were sometimes used for the gardens. Once he had gone there was the cleaning to be done. Even though all the furniture was covered up the soot managed to find its way in.'

## ⬧ Hard Times ⬧

'My story begins before I was born. Mr and Mrs Mallett were taking their usual walk through Aston Park and called in the little pub near the park gates, and whilst there Mrs Mallett heard the tales and fears of a panic-stricken girl behind the bar. The girl was pregnant, and she had been turned out of her home by her parents – God-fearing people and caretakers of a church in the Black Country. This kind of treatment happened in the 1920s. Mrs Mallett in her impulsive, kind way was concerned for the girl and said, "Bring it to me if it's a girl." Some time later the girl – known only as Polly – arrived at Mrs Mallett's door in Park Road, Aston, carrying a bundle – a baby – ready to "make a hole in the river", and so at seven days old I was born again to Mr and Mrs Mallett, who I always called Mom and Dad and I took their name. Polly was taken in too and restored to better health and able to look for work. She never returned, though there was an occasional letter and a meeting when I was about three years old.

My adopted parents were not the average couple, Dad was 33 years older than my Mom. He was a businessman, broken by the First World War, a widower with three daughters, all married and they were not pleased when he married a working class widow with a son, left homeless. He needed a house-keeper, she needed a home, but they made a very fine respectable couple.

By the time I was older we were in real poverty, much to Dad's great dismay and perhaps his bewilderment because he had known a very different way of life. Mom nursed him in his last illness, hardly leaving him during those six months, except to try and earn the odd shilling doing washing and cleaning, sometimes for his daughters or her own sister. There was no "income support" in those days no matter how hard up you were and no doctor's notes. The house Dad took when his business failed was a good house but the rent of eleven shillings per week took some finding, and it went up twopence or threepence each year.

Mom took work wherever it was to be found in the factories that were so numerous in Birmingham in those days, and then came home to do her sister's washing and cleaning as well as our own home. When I was about five years old, Mom brought back with her from the "Yard" where her sister lived, two boys, Johnny and Arthur. Their mother had left them with their father and gone back to her mother in Luton taking her two daughters with her. Mom had found the boys sitting on top of the few sticks of furniture when the landlord had turned them out of the house after non-payment of the meagre rent, probably while their father was in the lock-up, drunk. The young one, Arthur, was only about two and a half years, Johnny five years older, so I acquired two brothers. Poor old Dad! They were lousy and only had the few poor clothes on their backs.

Somehow Mom did manage and had to deal with the monster of a father from time to time. Then work was hard to get and she had to apply for parish relief. How this degrading time must have devastated Dad. These relief people of course wanted to know all about the children and the result was the two boys were taken from Mom. They were put into a home which I believe was in Spring Hill. I can recall visiting them as Mom fought to get them back.

Mom did get them back again after a long battle, and we all once again did our little jobs to help to keep the home going. Mom worked at one time at a factory in the middle of Birmingham, hard work, motor flatting, I think it was called, rubbing down the metal sheets which made the mudguards for the Austin Works which was then the beginning of the motor industry.

The lady owner, Mrs Crossley, was a kind lady I should think as Mom always thought well of her. I remember she gave her workers a beautiful powder compact with her portrait on the front, a lovely looking lady. The extra money would have been more use, but I don't expect she could appreciate the real need of some of her workers.'

# THE HOUSES WE LIVED IN

*N*o *electric light or heat, no running water, no indoor sanitation – running a household was a hard task (and probably never more so than on washday!) but we were all in the same boat and thought nothing of it in those gaslit days!*

### ⬛ A MINER'S COTTAGE ⬛

'I was born in 1915 and lived in a miner's cottage at Leighswood, Aldridge with my family until 1941. It is the early days I remember, when the daily jobs, or chores, were a ritual. Clearly, I can see my father getting up at 5 am to get to the pit for 6 am to check the "workings" before the miners went down to get the coal.

The first thing he did every morning was to crack the raker (a large lump of coal) on the fire and rake out the ashes to get a blazing fire going – as the kettle of water had been on the hob by the fire all night, the water soon boiled for the first cup of tea.

Lighting in the cottages was first by candles and oil lamps and later on there was a simple supply of gas (only downstairs) when we had gas lights on wall brackets or through a pipe hanging from the ceiling – the supply was controlled by a simple "on-off" tap and it was just too bad if you touched the mantle, which disintegrated. We did, as time went on, have a gas cooker, made of cast iron, standing on four legs. There was no bottom in the oven and the burners were at the bottom; the grids for cooking tins were above the burners so I presume it worked on the principle that heat rises – you had to guess when the oven was hot enough to use. On the top of the cooker there were burners and a peculiar contraption for grilling. This consisted of two flat plates with a central bar burner – in the middle was a little handle which, if you turned it one way turned the plates to throw the heat down for grilling, if you turned it the other way the heat came from the top for cooking or warming.

You washed in cold water taken from the rainwater butt outside or from the cold water tap – this too was outside sometimes. My mother's day was very different from today – each morning the brass knob and knocker on the front door were "rubbed up" and the front door step was washed and whitened with a bath brick.

Monday was always washday. All the cleaning in those days was done by hand, using brooms or mops and often scrubbing brushes, when you knelt down on an old coat or a pad to clean the quarries (tiles) and also the wooden floors in the bedrooms.

Working in the house was very time consuming as meals had to be prepared and cooked using mostly the range or fireplace in the kitchen or living room. Most women made bread and the dough was made early, left to rise (or prove) and covered over – the bowl (or jowl) was put near the fire before the dough was finally kneaded and baked in the oven at the side of the fire.

In between times there were pigs to feed and water and clean out and the hens had to be fed too and the eggs collected – not to mention the shopping in the village.'


### ▧  AN OLD FARMHOUSE NEAR COVENTRY  ▧

'I was born the fifth child in an old farmhouse in 1907, in the parish of Allesley, near Coventry. It was a long house, one room width except for the back kitchen. There was a huge dairy, with a thrawl on each side and one running down the middle, on one end of the house. Then the kitchen where we lived, into the hall, into the dining room from where the stairs ran. Through the dining room into a passage from where there was a butler's pantry, into a far room which was not furnished which was the last room in the long house.

Upstairs there was a bedroom at each end of the house and a passage running from them with four bedrooms and the stairs and a small room over the combined fireplaces of the kitchen and dining room. The room over the fireplaces was always warm and we kept all the bedlinen in there. We children used to race up and down the passage. One room was called the "cheese room". Former residents had made cheese and the floor, which was oak, smelled of stale cheese. We hated sleeping in that room but we had to when we had a lot of visitors. We also had back stairs which the workmen used to get to another bedroom which was theirs.

In the back kitchen there was a door into the brick oven. This was built out into the garden. Mother cooked bread occasionally. We filled the oven with branches and any wood we had and even rubbish and burned it. This heated the bricks which stayed hot a long time.

Each day we had to pump water into a large tank over the cooling shed. This water was then run through a cooler over which the milk ran into a churn. The milk was collected each morning. Sometimes it was taken to Tile Hill station in the horse and float. We had a "milk book" which showed we had 4½d per gallon for the milk and ½d taken off for carriage. We had ten each day for Mother to cater for: Mother, Father, a cousin who lived with us, five children and two men who "lived in".

Two pigs were killed each year. Father salted the bacon in one of the thrawls. We had two or three 60lb cheeses from Cheshire each year (Mother was a farmer's daughter and had made cheese).

On washday I have heard Mother say she dare not leave the ironing for another day because each brought its own work, so she would often be ironing at 1 am. We girls wore frilled knickers, petticoats, dresses and pinafores and Father wore starched collars, cuffs and shirt fronts. Boys wore girls' clothes much longer in those days and it was quite an occasion when they were put into trousers. My brother wore knee breeches and starched collars.

Our range was used for everyday cooking on one side and we put in sticks to dry for lighting. These were put in each evening. We had a fender which Mother cleaned with ashes and spit and the range was cleaned with black lead. The fire itself was high and most of the heat went up the chimney. We lived in the kitchen and it was very cold. Father did all he could to keep out the draughts but often we put on our coats in the evenings.'

## ▧ GASLIGHT UNTIL 1963 ▧

'In 1908 my grandmother died in London, and wished to be buried in the same grave as her son, who had died whilst working in Birmingham. Accordingly her coffin was brought by train from Southwark and she was buried in Yardley cemetery.

My mother and grandfather, being left alone, decided to leave London and come to Birmingham to live near the cemetery. They were able to find a private house (at that time all houses were rented privately from the landlord) to rent, near Little Bromwich and Bordesley Green. My grandfather found work in the building trade and my mother as a daily domestic help in the large houses in Acocks Green, at one shilling per morning from 9 am until 2 pm.

Then Mother was married, the Great War broke out in August 1914, and my father, a Territorial, volunteered, as they all did, for service overseas. I was born and when I was 17 months old my father was killed on the Somme. Mother was a widow for 56 years. Money was very short in those war years and after. I remember skimmed condensed milk, margarine, rice pudding.

I also remember the copper in the "combined kitchen" of our house, this meant a kitchen and scullery combined. The fire was lit under the copper boiler, to boil the water to wash the clothes, cold water being put in from the tap. The boiler was then emptied by hand. The mangle was a wonderful thing to get water out of the clothes, especially the sheets. There was a coal-fire range with an oven which was supposed to cook the food when the fire was lit, but it never did, also a large cupboard, a flat sink, a black gas oven with two burners on top (the gas oven was on loan from the gas department) and the floor was red flat large bricks, called "quarries". All floors

*Natural Gas arrives in Coleshill in August 1968.*

were cleaned by kneeling down and scrubbing them, linoleum included.

The second reception room was dark, had a black Victorian fireplace, which had to be blackleaded, and the stairs to the upper floor went out of one corner. Then there was the front room, with a bay window and a lovely black marble fireplace surround, cornices and rose over the gas light in the centre of the room. We had gas light in this house until 1963 when my mother paid to have the electricity put in. A friend up the road had gas light until 1980.'

'Until I was 18, my parents' home was lit by gas. The gas was supplied through a meter, situated at the base of the coal cellar steps.

Meters took old pennies or shillings, and some, not ours, were quarterly ones. Imagine during cooking one's meal the gas cutting off, or the light dimming. Someone would have to go down the cellar steps to feed the coins into the meter to restore harmony above stairs. The short journey to dispatch the coins was illuminated by carrying a lit candle, torch, or even lighting a match, not a safe practice even today. The gas light was activated by first pulling down one of two chains, on and off, then lighting the gas mantle with a match, or spill, lit from the coal fire. Sometimes by being heavy-handed lighting the mantle it had a hole punctured into it, resulting in the light flickering for evermore.

The first and second storeys of our home were equipped with gas pipes, but the attic bedroom, which I shared with my sister, again relied on candlelight, torch or a paraffin lamp, called a Kelly lamp. All these lighting forms cast shadows on the walls, which when a child used to scare me half to death.

In those pre-television days, our one and only radio relied on an accumulator and battery for power. The gramophone, on the other hand, was spring-loaded, and required a cranking-handle to activate it.

To return to when I was 18, my parents decided to move into the house next door, which had electricity installed in 1931. It seemed like a dream, instant light! But being 17 years old, the house was already old-fashioned and in need of some improvements. We still did not have a bathroom, but we had wonderful, easily-obtained electricity.'


## ▦ AN UPSTAIRS BATHROOM! ▦

'I was born in 1924 in Pelsall in a house designed by my mother and father. We had two living rooms, a kitchen, an outside coalhouse, three large bedrooms and – very rare in the village then – an upstairs bathroom! I often accompanied my father when he visited people in the village either on chapel or legal business, so I was able to see the interior of some of the large mid-Victorian houses with their oak panelling, Turkish carpets, red plush curtains, oak block floors and Minton tiled passages.

In 1860 a large ironworks had been built on the North Common next to the canal, bringing new prosperity to the village. The new houses of that time were mainly terraced with two bedrooms, two living rooms – one serving as the kitchen, washroom and Friday night bathroom. Outside was the brewhouse and bakery, an ash pit, an earth closet (often shared) and a pig sty. Many houses had a cellar, used for curing bacon, storing fruit, vegetables and beer, and keeping butter cool in summer. I've sat in my grandparents' cellar many times to cool off on hot summer days.'

## ▣ CHILBLAINS ▣

'In 1927 in Small Heath, Birmingham, my family lived in what was called a villa-type residence. There were whole roads of them. You had an entry between two houses and the other side you were joined to another house, but it wasn't exactly a semi-detached because the bedrooms adjoined over the entry, if you know what I mean.

That house, it had a long tiled hall which was so cold it used to chill your blood. I remember Jack Frost on the windowpane in the winter, bedsocks and chilblains. We undressed downstairs by the fire and even if you wanted to go to the loo you hung on and hung on because it meant leaving the fireside to go out in the cold. My mother always had cracks on the front of her legs from sitting by the fire and I had chilblains so I could hardly get my shoes on. We used that green block for them, Snowfire – some people would put their feet in a full chamberpot and that was supposed to cure chilblains.'

## ▣ A TERRACE IN BIRMINGHAM ▣

'Grandmother's terraced house, which was in the Vauxhall district of Birmingham, had two rooms upstairs and two rooms down; no bathroom and the lavatory at the end of the garden. There was a black-leaded range with high mantelpiece and a small gas cooker. Lighting was by gas and when lighting the gas you had to be careful not to pierce the mantle with the match.

The wireless was run by accumulator and this had to be taken to a local shop for recharging. I can't remember them but Mother used to talk about the first wirelesses which were called crystal sets and apparently one had to move a piece of wire, called a cat's whisker, over a stone until the station was found. She said her elder brother used to pay her for doing this!

The front room of the house was kept very tidy and was only used on Sundays and holidays. There was a horsehair sofa and when you sat on it, it scratched your legs. There was a scrubbed wooden table covered by a chenille tablecloth.

Grandmother wore long dresses covered by a huge pinafore and black button boots which she fastened with a button hook. For hard work she used to wear a hurden (thick sacking) apron.

We used to eat stew, bread pudding, bread and dripping or bread and lard. On Sundays an Italian man came round on a bike selling ice cream, and a man with a basket carriage selling periwinkles which you ate after they had been removed from the shell with a pin.

In the bedroom there was a large brass bed with knobs on. There was a wooden chest of drawers and clothes were stored behind a curtain in the recess by the side of the fireplace. There were wooden floorboards and peg rugs on each side of the bed.'

## ▣ RECYCLING ▣

'The word "recycling" wasn't known to our parents' generation but the process certainly was. Almost everything in our house was recycled with the exception of members of the family.

Brown paper and string were carefully removed from parcels and saved. Paper bags from shops were smoothed, folded and put away. The insides of used envelopes and the backs of Christmas cards were set aside for notes and shopping-lists. Newspapers had a myriad of re-uses – for covering a newly-washed floor; for making wet parcels of coal-slack to put at the back of the grate; for wrapping fragile objects such as eggs and fine china in transit; for stuffing into the toes of new boots bought a size too big to allow for growth and of course, for cutting into those neat squares which were to be found hung up on a nail in every dry closet. On the rare occasions when new linoleum was bought, the floorboards were first covered with thick layers of newspaper.

All the waste from the garden, the hen-houses and the kitchen went into the midden. Rhubarb leaves were excepted since they were believed to be poisonous. To this was added the contents of the dry closet, well covered with soil, to await the coming of spring. When J was a child this thought occasionally bothered me when I was eating potatoes.

Tins were put to one side and pieces were cut out to deal with a variety of repair jobs on the out-buildings. The remains, and they didn't amount to much since little tinned food was bought, were beaten flat and buried.

The planks used to repair a shed or even to build a new one frequently showed old nail-holes. Old iron bed-ends did duty as gates or filled gaps in fences.

Secondhand railway sleepers provided a cheap and ready source of timber. Old carriages were also available and can still be seen acting as hen-houses, stores or even village cricket pavilions. A childhood friend lived in a comfortable cottage made from two such carriages. They had been placed parallel to one another and about twelve feet apart. A stone wall was built across the space between to accommodate two back-to-back fireplaces and to carry the pitched roof over the whole area. A living room was constructed on either side of this wall. Each carriage was cut across by an interior wall thus providing three bedrooms and a kitchen. The original let-down windows were left in place, still with their leather straps. An outer timber "skin" enclosed the whole.

It was in clothing and household linen that recycling really came into its own. After all the mending, patching, taking in, letting out, shortening, lengthening, handing down and wearing out, the remains were put away for further use. This would include supplying more patches, making dusters and floor-cloths according to material, giving strips for hooked hearthrugs and pieces to form long "sausages" to keep the draughts out. "Good" skirts and jackets were taken to the local dressmaker to be turned. This involved taking the garment apart and remaking it.

Household linen was also patiently patched and darned before being consigned to baser uses. Sheets having been turned sides-to-middle were finally cut up to make pillowslips. The smallest pieces were kept for dealing with cuts or for cleaning-rags. Pillow-cases, worn very thin, made soft bits for blowing sore noses during winter colds. New pillowcases were often made from the strong white flour-bags which the baker sold for sixpence. They lasted for ever. They were boiled thoroughly and bleached to remove the print although this wasn't always successful. The best bits of towels were cut and hemmed for face-cloths.

Knitted garments were the most profitable. The unravelled wool – and it was wool in those days – was hanked, washed, dried and wound into balls to be reknitted into smaller jumpers and cardigans. Again it was unpicked to reappear as mittens or socks. The remains of these were fashioned into house-slippers for the children. In the end all that could be salvaged was wound, several different strands together, into huge balls and kept until there was enough to knit or crochet a bed-cover. This in its turn ended up outside, covering the old garden seat before making bedding for the dog kennel or protecting potatoes from the frost.

Fathers repaired the family footwear as far as they were able. Most households possessed a cobbler's last – a heavy metal object of an awkward shape with three different-sized "feet" sticking out at odd angles – for this purpose. The walls of discarded car tyres were cut into the appropriate shape and nailed onto worn soles. Warm insoles were made from old felt hats.

Rabbits were a cheap source of protein for poor families and their skins were collected by the local rag-man for recycling. He paid two-pence or threepence a skin. Eggshells were crushed finely and fed back to the hens. Feathers were kept for pillows and cushions. Left-overs from the family table were given to the dogs and cats – no tinned pet food then. A dog's dinner really looked like one.

Even those old thick gramophone records were recycled by being warmed gently in the oven and formed into fluted bulb bowls.

The wartime radio experts who held forth about make do and mend were preaching to the converted in most working class homes. That was where the real experts were to be found.'

### ◈ WASHDAY MEMORIES ◈

'Most Sunday evenings today I put my washing into a machine, I choose a programme and press a button. In my youth in the 1920s what a difference. Washday was a two person job. Each Sunday evening the clothes were sorted into piles across the yard and the boiler filled with water. One bucket was filled with a solution of Rinso and in it the very soiled clothes were left overnight. We got up at six o'clock on Monday to light the boiler and get breakfast over and the beds made early, then we started.

All whites went into the hot water and there was a careful wash of the woollens, these were rinsed twice and hung out to dry. Then the boiled clothes were lifted out with some heavy wooden tongs into a tub for the first rinse, while a further lot of whites were boiling. After possing the first lot with a posser, no light job, there was another rinse and through the mangle. Some were hung out to blow while others waited for the starch.

About ten o'clock we broke off for a cup of tea. During this break we made the starch and prepared the blue water. You made a paste with cold water and a large spoonful of Robin's powdered starch then poured on boiling water from the kettle until it broke, at this point the white paste cracked into a grey gluey mess!

Across the yard again to starch and blue some of the whites and fold carefully through the heavy mangle. Then out again into the garden with the pegs. After the last lot of the boilings, including dusters and floor-cloths, we did the few silks. Then everywhere was scrubbed clean, the mangle rollers released and the water poured from the boiler onto the concrete floor. The windows and doors were left open to help everything to dry while we had our dinner.

Our meal was always the cold joint from Sunday and chipped potatoes. Then off again to collect from the line whatever was dry. At first we had two flat irons and worked on the kitchen table but eventually we had an electric iron and what joy that was! When we had a good blowing wind we could be finished by four o'clock, but have a wet day and the kitchen would be full of wet clothes until Tuesday and we had to rise early again to try and catch up because Tuesday was also a very busy day. I don't think anyone would work so hard now.'

'Water had to be carried from a communal tap in some homes in Streetly, while others had cold water only on tap and heated it on the fire or stove. Table linen and other cotton items including shirt collars were dipped in a bowl of starch. Men wore shirts with detachable collars; the shirt would be worn all week and the collar was changed two or three times during the week!

Flat irons were heated on the fire or on the gas stove, then placed in a metal holder, held firm with brackets. The ironed clothes were placed on a wooden clothes horse to air near the fire. Larger items were hung up on a rack in the kitchen. This was suspended near the ceiling and lowered by ropes. Many homes sent clothes out to be laundered, either to a laundry or to a local woman who took in washing.'

## THE COKE RATION

'Every Saturday morning I would go down to Saltley Gasworks to collect the coke ration for our families. I was eleven years old and we lived in Cato Street North. I would push the four-wheeled cart my Dad made for me. I earned the grand sum of threepence for every trip I made. At the end of the morning when I had finished I went up to my Aunt Violet's, and she always had a hot breakfast waiting for me, bacon bits and fried tomatoes with fresh crusty bread – smashing!'

## GRANNY'S WASHING

'I loved helping Granny to hang out her washing. My task was to hold up the pegs. When she had finished, I liked to look at her underwear on the line. It was so different from my mother's and it was all home-made. There was a loose garment called a chemise. Then came her "bust-bodice", a sort of short, close-fitting top, darted to her shape and fastening down the front with linen buttons. The petticoat was simple. It was ankle-length and tied round the waist with tape. The most fascinating sight was what she called her "drawers". These consisted of two long legs attached to a waistband which buttoned at the back. The legs were seamed together, front and back for a few inches below the waist and again from just above the knee to the foot where they were finished with bands edged with broderie anglaise. Today they would be referred to as "open-crotch". She showed me how she kept her stockings up. She rolled the top down to below the knee and tucked a penny into this roll. Then she twisted the penny until the stocking-top was tight against her leg and pushed the penny up again into the roll. Toward the end of her life she abandoned her "drawers" for black Celanese "bloomers".'

# FOOD AND SHOPPING

*We lived on what we grew or made for the most part and for many people that meant home-cured bacon and fresh pork from the pig kept in the garden sty! There seemed more time then, and shopping was a pleasure and a sociable occasion – and of course we had so much delivered to our doors!*

## ◙ WE LIVED ON WHAT WE GREW ◙

'In Allesley in 1907 we had bread brought to the door twice a week in a high, horse-drawn trap but Mother did most of the cooking. We often took our own corn to be ground at a local mill and we had a large flour bin into which we emptied it in the dairy. During the First World War we lived on what we grew, eggs, fowl, pigs and garden produce. Our ration of sugar was half a pound each a week. Mother weighed out a quarter pound each for our use and the rest she kept for cooking. We had a large orchard full of all sorts of fruit trees. We were teetotallers but Mother made a drink called Mason's Extract, lemonade with citric acid, and a sort of ginger beer. This was taken to the men in harvest time. Father preferred cold tea with a raw egg beaten into it.'

## ◙ PIGS, BEER AND WATERCRESS ◙

'Besides making wine (parsnip was my favourite), my grandparents brewed their own beer; it was dark in colour, rather like Guinness.

From an early age I was given this "pop" in a half pint glass inscribed "J. Fox, Freetrade Inn, Pelsall". He was my great great grandfather. It was always possible to tell who was brewing; the smell hung around for days.

Most people at Pelsall in the 1920s kept a pig in the sty at the top of the garden. Squeals and shouts told us when the poor beast was being killed, usually in the backyard. Boiling of pig's trotters and chitterlings and rendering of lard would keep Grandma busy for days, and the smell was vile. But how I enjoyed the lard on a piece of toast with a glass of ale when I called in on my way home from school.

On Saturday afternoons an old lady in black used to visit the village pushing a large wicker basket on wheels. She had walked all the way from Sutton Park where she had picked watercress from one of the pools. The stems were wide enough to use as drinking straws. What flavour!'

## ❖ Killing the Pig ❖

'This indeed was a very important occasion in our house in the late 1930s when I was a girl.

We kept the pig in a brick-built pigsty at the bottom of the garden which overlooked open country fields. The pig was killed during the evening as usually the butcher had to work during the day. We had no brothers – so we girls would have to hold the lantern while the deed was done.

But how well we ate! My mother would make the most delicious faggots from the liver and fry – the like of which I have never tasted since. Two leafs of lard made two bowls of snowy white fat. She also made a boney pie from ribs, bones, pastry and potatoes and lovely brawn from the pig's cheeks.

My father would put on an apron and sit at our kitchen table making the pork pies. The flitches of bacon he would salt by hand down in our cellar. They were not put in baths of brine like they are today. Many families provided food for themselves in this and other ways.'

## ◈ ANIMAL MEMORIES ◈

'My earliest memories of the 1920s all seem to be connected with animals. My first memory is of my own pet bantam called Rita, which insisted she laid her eggs in my dolls' pram; there too she hatched a clutch of chicks and was regularly pushed around the garden.

My father had a mixed farm so there were seasonal events. Calves were born, which resulted in puddings made from the second and third milking after calving (called beastings). Further milk was set in pans, cream was skimmed off and each week churned to make butter, for home use or made up into attractive half pound pats for sale.

Lambs arrived and if the weather was very cold we had to bring them indoors to warm them. My mother sat in front of an open fire with a hessian sack folded over her knees and a piece of old blanket to wrap around the lamb and keep warming until it looked more likely to survive.

Pigs brought problems too. As far as possible draughts were excluded with straw from their pens where the sows were to farrow. A hurricane lantern was used for light and warmth and if possible there was someone in attendance. If necessary the same treatment was used for weakling and cold piglets as the lambs. It was important every one was saved. It was our livelihood and more good food would be around when the bacon pigs were slaughtered.

That was a busy time. We cleaned the belly as soon as it was out of the pig and turned it each day for four days. The bladder was blown up and dried out for tying down pickles. There was lard to be made, also black pudding, faggots, brawn, pork pies and a boney pie. In the meantime the sides of bacon and hams were being cured with common salt over a period of three weeks.'


## ◈ A GREAT DEAL OF TIME! ◈

'We seemed to spend a great deal of our time eating. For breakfast my mother dished up bacon, egg, fried tomatoes, fried potatoes and a slice of fried bread, and then tipped hot fat over it all "to dip your bread in"! Dinner was always meat and two veg, followed by a pudding with custard. Then tea – bread and jam or fish paste, and cake or Harvo loaf smothered in butter. And we'd finish the day with supper: bread and cheese and a cup of Ovaltine.'

'My childhood was spent in a mining town, so I awoke to the sound of miners walking to work, their clogs making clinking sounds on the hard road. A lovely coal fire would already be burning in the shining, blackleaded grate, having been kept in all night. Breakfast began with porridge cooked in the oven in a brown earthenware jar, followed by bacon sizzling in the Dutch oven – a pan which was put on a trivet in front of the fire. The food to be cooked was hung on hooks in the pan. When one side of the food was cooked it was possible to turn the oven over to cook the other side. Eggs would be cooked in the bottom of the pan at the same time. Home baking was general in those days and the lovely smell of freshly baked bread wafted round the kitchen.'

## ▨ HOLIDAYS WITH GRANNY ▨

'Most of my early childhood memories in the 1930s were of holidays I spent with my Granny.

In the morning the milkman delivered milk with his horse and cart. He would fill our milk jugs from his churn – using a metal pint pot to measure it. This he hung on the side of the churn. No such things as bottles and pasteurised milk!

The coal was delivered by (literally) coal-black men who carried the sacks on their backs and threw them down the chute into the coal cellar, with a most satisfying noise. The other half of the big cellar was Granny's "fridge". Marble slabbed and cool, it would keep many things fresh. Nearly always, there were two great pancheons filled with a spicy and slightly sour smelling liquid with yeast-spread slices of bread floating on the top. This was destined to be bottled and become delicious ginger beer. One day a dreadful noise was heard from the cellar – one of the bottles had exploded and the cellar was sticky with ginger beer.

From the range on Thursday came the week's baking – bread, tea cakes and pies. Any dough left over was made into lardy cakes – sandwiched with butter and raisins and scattered with brown sugar.

I had a job to do. They had an ancient knife sharpener in the pantry and I had to put the knives head down in the slots and turn the wheel, and hopefully they turned out sharp. I also had to grate the salt, which was bought in large blocks.'

### ▨ Shopping Days ▨

'Shops were much more restful, usually with a chair provided for the customer.

The butcher would greet you in a straw hat, and have sawdust liberally spread on the floor. Grocers' shops were a delight. Everything was weighed, from biscuits to butter, butter being patted and cut into shape, with often the impression of a thistle or cow on the front. Little pokes of paper were used to hold small items, often coming out of small wooden drawers behind the counter. Bacon

*The milkman delivered straight from the churn in the 1920s.*

would be sliced to the thickness you desired, and a small piece of cheese offered to approve the flavour. The bill would then be totted up, money produced and all put in a small metal cylinder on a wire, which with a lovely ping would shoot across the shop to a lady in an office at the back.

In all shops would hang flypapers, and disastrous it was if a blue-bottle had reached your bacon.

Later that day, orders would be delivered by a boy on a bicycle with a large metal basket in front and the name of the shop hanging from the crossbar.'


### ▨ DELIVERED TO THE DOOR ▨

'Provisions were delivered by horse-drawn vehicles. The milkman was often late, especially on foggy mornings, because first he had to find the horse, harness it and then load the crated bottles. He always gave the horse his nosebag outside our bungalow because Mother gave him an early-morning cuppa and sandwich. One of us was sent with a galvanised bucket and a spade to "watch for the results" as horse manure was much sought after to use on the vegetable gardens. Sometimes the horse had wandered and my friends would claim the prize as theirs as it had been deposited outside their house.

Bread came in a horse-drawn van. It was often still hot or warm, large white loaves still unbroken in long wooden trays. The baker's man had a long wooden pole with a square hook on the end, with which he pulled bread to the back of the van to put into his colossal wicker basket. Then he would trudge up the garden path to the back door. Often I would be sent with a message to the gate to save his legs, and if there was a loaf with a crust at only one end I would steal soft bread from the other and eat it on the way back, it was so tasty.'

'Shopping for food, right up into the 1960s, was a daily chore. Meat was delivered three times a week at my home in the 1930s, and fruit and vegetables came by horse and cart. The local Co-operative Society delivered bread and milk by horse and cart. As a young mother in 1958 I would stand with my small son waiting for the Co-op horse to deliver the bread and cakes.'

Phone: Tanworth-in-Arden 346

*Ansells*

DR. TO

# T. G. MONK

"ROYAL OAK"
WOOD END, HOCKLEY HEATH,
NEAR BIRMINGHAM,

........ 7 August ........ 195 7

M— *Hicks* .

| | | | | |
|---|---|---|---|---|
| 3 | Vin Sherry | 2 | 14 | 0 |
| 1 | " Port | | 18 | 0 |
| 1 | Booths Gin | 1 | 14 | 6 |
| 18 | Nut Brown Ale | 1 | 10 | 0 |
| 6 | Spec | | 8 | 3 |
| 1 | Syphon | | 5 | 3 |
| 12 | Sun Tang | | 10 | 0 |
| 12 | Lemon | | 8 | 0 |
| 6 | Tonic | | 4 | 0 |
| | £ | 8 | 12 | 0 |
| | | | 2 | 4 |
| | £ | 8 | 14 | 4 |

*A bill for drinks from August 1957, including £1 10s for the Nut*
*Brown Ale.*

69

'When I was a little girl, Monday morning was a social occasion. The grocer would cycle up and be seated in the kitchen, while my mother gave her grocery order for the week. This took some while, as we were a family of six, and Mr Thompson would wait patiently while she thought, sometimes making suggestions if he thought she had forgotten an essential item. When the business was completed, the woman who came in to help with the washing was called up from the cellar, and all would be regaled with a cup of cocoa and slices of buttered tea cake.

On Monday afternoon, when Mother went to meet the older children from school, she would call at the shop to pay for her order and would sit down at the counter whilst the bill was added up, and would be plied with tasters of a special type of cheese perhaps, or a new variety of biscuit.

On Tuesday morning the errand boy would appear with our box of groceries on his delivery bicycle. How times have changed!'

## ◫ On Caldmore Green ◫

'There was Ellis's bakehouse which I passed every day. They baked the most delicious bread in the world to my way of thinking. They had their own shop, so the bread was carried fresh into the shop each day and smelled simply wonderful. Ellis's employed a lovely character called Dick, who not only baked the bread, but also took out the horse and cart and delivered it. The horse and cart were kept in the cobbled yard where the ovens were – I suppose it would be considered unhygienic today – and Dick was groom as well. At Christmas time Ellis's would give Dick permission to keep the ovens going and cook turkeys for any family in the street wishing to use his services. My mother, having seven mouths to feed, and a turkey too big for our oven, would take it in a roasting tin, very early on Christmas morning, up the street to the bakehouse, and collect it several hours later. I can see her now, carrying it through the front door, and yes, I can smell it too.

On Caldmore Green we also had various butchers' shops. They had their meat delivered on the hoof, so we would see the cows, sheep, and pigs delivered. As children, we thoroughly enjoyed seeing the pigs driven up the entry of the pork butcher (the thought horrifies me today) and when the occasional one got loose and was chased until it was caught, there would be squeals of delight mingled with the squeals from the unfortunate pig.

I remember too the man who came round the streets with a contraption with which he sharpened knives and scissors. This machine would be on wheels, and have a grinding stone attached to a treadle. The man would treadle furiously, the grinding stone spun round, and sparks would fly as he sharpened our utensils.'

## ▧ ALL DRESSED UP ▧

'My mother would never dream of going shopping unless she was well dressed – shoes highly polished, clothes brushed and stocking seams straight.'

## ▧ RATION DAY AT THE Co-op ▧

'In the late 1940s Thursday was ration day at the Co-op. As a child I was fascinated by the cashier in a little cubicle set above the counter and the wonderful system of ropes and pulleys that whizzed the money round the shop. My ambition was to be a Co-op cashier when I grew up! I was always given a piece of cheese to nibble as we moved round the shop filling our order. My mother had a list and knew down to the last farthing how much everything cost.

Because meat was rationed, many women tried to get a bit extra from the butcher by saving their newspapers for him to wrap the meat in.'

## ▧ NEVER AGAIN! ▧

'It was 1934, the time of the wedding of the Duke of Kent and Princess Marina. Lewis's in Birmingham had a wedding cake and I went with my aunt to see it. This was also the time when Lewis's had just had escalators installed. We needed to go to a higher floor and decided to try out this moving stair. The sides of the staircase were of solid wood with a moving band on the top where you put your hand to steady yourself. My aunt, however, put her hand on the wooden side. Her feet went up with the stair, her hand and upper body stayed put. She was doing a sort of marking time and was completely unable to get herself upright and regain her balance. Lewis's had to stop the escalator. My aunt's reaction: "I am never going on one of those again!" She didn't.'

## FROM THE CRADLE TO THE GRAVE

*We were far more likely to be born, to suffer our illnesses and to die in our own homes in the past, and home cures were passed down through the generations and relied on to get us through most crises. However, childhood illnesses were often deadly and so many of us remember the fever epidemics and isolation hospitals of our youth.*

### ▨ CEMETERY OINTMENT ◈

'My younger sister and I had the usual milder children's ailments, but much more serious diseases were prevalent such as diphtheria and whooping cough. The killer diseases common among adults were tuberculosis, pneumonia and "miners' dust". The word cancer was rarely used and salmonella poisoning never heard of, perhaps through wrong diagnosis as hygiene in many food shops was primitive. After cutting a steak the butcher thought a quick wipe of his knife on his apron sufficed before slicing boiled ham off the bone. One baker had a cat sleeping about his shop and when baking started at dusk, cockroaches swarmed up the walls. The place was festooned with flypapers, rarely changed, and dead flies dropping onto food were idly flicked away. Understandably, stomach-ache was common, usually remedied with a spoonful of brandy.

Villagers tended to treat less serious complaints themselves. An ancient cousin told me that the cemetery keeper in Bloxwich had his own cure-all for cuts, bruises and skin complaints. It was based on a variety of ivy which grew on headstones. The local chemist made this up into a greasy paste, put it into small round cardboard boxes and sold it at a penny a time. It was known as "Cemetery Ointment".'


## ⬚ Home Remedies ⬚

'One way to cure a wart was to rub it with a piece of beef steak and then take the meat to the very bottom of the garden and bury it. The wart was supposed to wither away within a few days.

For an abscess on a tooth it was recommended to place a hot cooked prune inside the mouth by the affected area.

If roadmenders were encountered, it was thought beneficial to the chest to get a good lung full of the fumes from the tar lorry.'

'Father used to have lumbago. Mother once ironed his back with brown paper, which was supposed to be a cure. He said he was never nearer hitting Mother. I suppose the iron was too hot.

One sister woke up my parents coughing. She was put into a warm bath and given ipecacuanha wine which made her sick and so saved her life.'

'When my mother was small, inoculation against smallpox was done at home by the local doctor. In the case of my uncle, my mother's little brother, the arm refused to heal afterwards. Every visit by the doctor had to be paid for and so was avoided if possible. For this reason, my grandmother consulted the village handy woman. She it was who delivered babies, laid out the dead and gave good advice on a variety of subjects. She advised my grandmother to send to the farm for good thick fresh cream, to spread it on a clean cloth and bind it on the arm. This my grandmother did, changing the dressing every day for the week specified. By then the arm was very much worse and my grandmother was angry. When she complained to her friend, she was told that she had misunderstood her instructions. She was to leave the cream on the arm for a week without touching it. "Until it stinks," said the woman. She did this and it worked like a miracle.

Out-buildings were commonly festooned with thick dust-laden cobwebs. Old folk called these "moose (mouse) wobs" in the belief that tiny things like spiders couldn't be responsible for their construction. In my paternal grandmother's childhood a handful of these webs would be held on a wound to stop the bleeding.

An old Orcadian woman told me that when she was young, a cure for a stomach upset was to induce the patient to eat a salt herring. She supposed that it worked because it led to the drinking of great quantities of water. I wonder if the sufferer declared himself cured in order to avoid having to eat a second salt herring.'

'Several decades ago and dubbed the young needlewoman of a family of seven children, I was always given the task of sewing squares of camphor into little muslin bags. These were then pinned on to our liberty bodice or vest, supposedly to ward off colds and other infections of childhood. In those days many of the latter led to serious illnesses and often proved fatal. For this fear and to our dismay, Mother would not allow us to join the local library or even borrow books from friends, germs were thought to lurk between the pages!

I well remember our wonderful father, who, in spite of no medical training, would line us up and syringe our ears, often with very painful results. Small wonder that in later years I was told that both ear drums were permanently scarred.

Mother used permanganate of potash crystals to make a bright purple liquid which was used for almost every ailment, from minor cuts and grazing to sore throats, skin rashes and also as an excellent disinfectant. It is interesting to note that an eminent skin specialist in the Midlands is now, once again, prescribing its use, rather more diluted, for certain types of skin troubles. How I wish Mother was around to say, "There, I told you so."'

'When my grandmother was young, little attention was given to children's teeth. By the time she was 30, she had five children and her teeth were in a very poor state. There was no local dentist so the doctor was called in. He came once a week and removed several teeth on each occasion. My grandmother sat on a kitchen chair in the window to get the best light. She tied a towel across her chest and held the washing up bowl in her lap. Many of the extractions required lancing of the gum and there was no anaesthetic.'


## ◙ SEWN IN ◙

'Even after the Second World War, some children in Stechford were still being sewn into their clothes for the winter, and money had to be put on the table in some areas before a doctor would treat a patient.'


## ◙ OUT OF SIGHT ◙

'Mentally ill people tended to be cared for at home by their relatives. There was quite a stigma attached to mental handicap and they were kept out of sight as much as possible. There was little help available for the families.

Common problems in those days were boils or carbuncles, possibly due to poor diet. Children always seemed to have dirty noses! They frequently had styes on their eyes or impetigo and of course head lice were rife. I remember my mother combed our hair once or twice a week with a fine-toothed comb and then we were shampooed with Durbac soap.'


## ◙ CHILDHOOD ILLNESS ◙

'How different in the 1940s from now. Most children seemed to catch most childhood ailments. After only a few weeks at school, aged five, I caught measles. This meant being confined to bed in a darkened room to combat any eye problems. All senses seemed to be attacked. As an only child particularly fond of reading it was purgatory. The day I was to be allowed back into the land of the living, out I came with mumps, contracted about the same time, I was told, but with a longer incubation period. Back to the room above and isolation plus a decoratively bandaged face for the swelling.

Next came whooping cough, very debilitating, weeks off school leaving a lasting "graveyarder" cough as my grandmother called it. It wasn't *true* whooping cough unless the doctor heard you "whoop" in your breath. Many nervous children held their breath at the doctor's and never coughed at all, having earlier reduced their families to nervous breakdowns with their noise.

Lastly for me chicken pox, and I was banished from my grandmother's, where I was staying and enjoying being spoiled, as I had teenage uncles who didn't want it! This time arms and legs were bandaged to prevent scratching. I was lucky – many friends caught polio, one to be ever after in a wheelchair. Even she was considered lucky, or luckier than some. I remember the town swimming pool closed in the hottest weather to avoid spreading polio when it was rife.

Hospital, however, I was glad never to visit as friends came home tearful, having had to leave behind treasured teddies, cuddly toys or books and games to avoid spreading infection. So you went in with tonsils and a favourite teddy and left both behind. Visitors were also not encouraged – what a difference now in children's wards.'

'When I was nearly ten years old in 1934, I developed scarlet fever just a week before Christmas. As I was an only child and the fever hospital was quite full, the doctor asked my mother if she would look after me at home. She agreed and received her instructions. I was to be isolated in my room for six weeks and a sheet soaked in Lysol disinfectant was to be hung across the doorway to deter any germs attempting to escape. I don't know how effective this was, but by today's standards it seems pretty primitive. My parents also washed in disinfected water after leaving my room.'

'At the age of five in 1931 I contracted diphtheria and was taken to Little Bromwich fever hospital where I spent the next five and a half months. The ward was part of a long single-storey building heated by a large open fire. Parents were not allowed to visit in those days. While I was away, my bedroom was fumigated and all the contents burnt.'

'If a child was unfortunate enough to be a victim of an epidemic such as poliomyelitis, or indeed to be crippled in any manner requiring hospitalisation for many months in an orthopaedic hospital, they could only be visited by their parents for one hour each week, on a Sunday from 2.30 to 3.30 pm. Even after long operations this rule applied, supposedly so the child would not be upset!'

## ❖ BIRTH, MARRIAGE AND DEATH ❖

'Births generally took place at home in our mining town, with a mid-wife in attendance. When the mother was able to leave the house, the first, visit was to be "churched" by arrangement with a local parson. Not to be churched before visiting other places was considered almost a sin.

Weddings were not such big affairs in those days. The wedding breakfast was held at home, attended by relatives and a few friends. A death in the family brought neighbours to the door offering their sympathies. They also had a collection to buy a wreath and many stood in line each side of the door as the coffin was brought out.'

'On 6th April 1948 my mother died. I was just 15 years old. As I was an only child, and my father worked in a factory on night shift, an aunt came from Ireland to help us when my mother took very ill, three weeks before she died.

My mother died at home, and as was the custom then, she was kept there until the funeral. I remember a neighbour coming in to help my aunt lay out the body. This was done by washing the body all over, then dressing her in a long white cotton nightdress, which had been kept for this occasion. A bandage was tied under the chin and round the head, in order to keep the mouth from dropping open, and her hair brushed and tidied. The bed was stripped and a clean white cotton sheet placed underneath the body, and one over the top. A white lace square was then placed over the face.

The following day, the coffin was taken upstairs and the body placed in it. The lid was left off until the day of the funeral. Four candles, brought by the Catholic priest, were placed at the corners of the bed; these were lit all night before the funeral. I was allowed to sleep at another aunt's house, who lived locally, while all the arrangements were made.

My father bought me a navy blue pin-striped suit to wear, and I

*A wedding in 1936, when huge bouquets were a fashionable accessory.*

had to sew a black band round the arm of my jacket, and one for my father. This also was the custom, a token of respect.

One thing I remember most vividly, was the confusion caused when the coffin was carried down the very narrow staircase and out of the house to the hearse. I think that was when I really realised my mother was dead.'

# CHILDHOOD&SCHOOLDAYS

# CHILDHOOD DAYS

*In town and country, our childhood days were freer than those of today's children. Hard times made many of us grow up quickly, though, particularly on the streets.*

### ⬧ BY THE CANAL ⬧

'Cruising along the canal in a modern "longboard" brought back memories of over 60 years ago when as a child I lived on the canal side. The clip-clop of horses' hooves on the two path heralded a colourful barge, sometimes trailing a butty boat behind, which cruised leisurely by with cheery greetings and waves from the family whom we all knew as friends.

Along the bank sat fishermen who had arrived from the city by motor train at the local station and walked along the lane to their chosen pitch hoping for a good day's catch – they were never too far away from the canal side pub (usually selling home brew) and beside the drawbridge which, if funds were low, my friends and I obligingly raised for the numerous pleasure boats cruising along in the warm sunshine (it never rained), all for an odd copper. We also helped "mine host" make and sell ice cream for the day trippers (delicious). Opposite the pub was a real gypsy caravan and family, forbidden to us as children. Each Saturday night after closing time the husband arrived home fighting drunk and incapable and the poor wife emerged next morning with a real shiner.

Should we decide it was time for a swim one of us walked along the tow path searching for dead dogs, cats, chickens etc in the water. If none was present we then dived into the water to swim with no thoughts of pollution. Although a car was not a possession of the households, they all had either rowing boat, punt or canoe – transport well used for visiting friends higher up the reach or for river picnics. Underneath the moored boats we could always expect to find a shoal of fish when we dropped our line or net. The wild life, flora and fauna we all accepted as a way of life, never realising that we were privileged to share the sight of the flight of a kingfisher diving for his supper.

We had such wonderful areas for playing a variety of games, making our own swings from the tree branches, sliding down the banks of the aqueduct, playing hide and seek, cycling, gathering mushrooms for breakfast and blackberries in season, and not forgetting scrumping. Whenever I hear (not often now) *In a Monastery Garden* or *In a Persian Market* it brings back the sound of the scraping of a neighbour's daughter learning to play the violin. We never seemed to be bored because the local farmers were very tolerant and encouraged us as we usually helped with harvesting.'

## TODDLING ROUND COVENTRY

'My memories are of the period 1925 to 1931, and of course the first couple of years of my life made no impression I can now recall. But I do have vivid recollections of a few things . . . walks on the fields now covered with the Mount Nod housing, huge hollows there we used to call "the Giant's washing up bowl", and hollow trees by the path that bad boys used to light fires in, and the terror of the gorse fires on Hearsall Common which I thought would spread up to our house and engulf it. The steamrollers trundling ever so slowly up and down the newly tarred roads, and the wonderful trams from Earlsdon Street into the city with top decks open at the front and back and the view of the Peeping Tom figure as you passed Greyfriars Green and entered Hertford Street – it was up in a window on the left.

My mother hardly ever took me with her to town, she was afraid of germs and also, no doubt, preferred to shop unimpeded by a straggling toddler so I was left in care of the charlady we had. But we went to church at Berkswell where I was removed before the sermon at matins lest I be restless and taken to look at the well which seemed in those days to have much more, much greener, moss all round it, and through the gates of the big house – then the vicarage as I seem to remember, one saw the vicar's black pug dogs waiting for his return from the service.

Other walks were from Broad Lane to Whoberley Avenue to visit

*Kathleen and Dorothy dressed in their Sunday best in 1918.*

family friends who had settled there – up Guphill on the right just near Broad Lane was a yew tree, the only one around. It is still there 60 years later and not noticeably bigger, but the pond with goldfish in the garden opposite has vanished, though the newsagent still functions at the Glendower Avenue/Broad Lane junction where I begged for copies of *Bo Peep*; my mother did not approve and told me I could only have one if I asked for it myself – which I usually failed to do in agonies of shyness! Another thing she hardly ever bought in response to my pleading were puff pastry tartlets full of confectioner's red jam or lemon curd, or the tiny Hovis miniature loaves, which tantalised me as we waited in Earlsdon for a tram to town on the rare occasions when she took me with her – or if we were shopping locally in that area. And I can just remember the bridle path down from Whoberley Avenue parallel to Glendower Avenue with Allesley Old Road at the bottom with a stream running along it and bridges over the stream.'

## ▨ THE MAGIC OF THE BULL RING ▨

'The Bull Ring in Birmingham was a fascinating and exciting place for a seven year old in 1948. My big brother Bryan used to take me there every Saturday morning. Hawkers with their wares and stallholders lined the hill leading down to the Bull Ring and St Martin's church. I can still remember the cries of some: "Kites for the kids, handy carriers, and steel wool for your pots, pans and aluminium."

It was all sheer magic to me, except for the stall which sold the tiny, fluffy yellow chicks, and the pet stalls in the market; I used to feel sorry for them all. At about the age of ten, my best friend Valerie and I went there on our own. Usually, I walked past the chicks' stall with my eyes screwed tightly together, but on one occasion I didn't, and ended up hurriedly buying two tiny balls of yellow fluff, despite protestations from Valerie telling me what I already knew – that my mother would be furious and that we had nowhere suitable to keep them in our very small crazy-paved back garden. I carried them carefully in one of the brown paper "handy carriers" and they chirped and whistled all the way home to the amusement of the bus conductor.

Valerie was right, my mother was horrified, but the chicks were delighted with their new found freedom, and immediately claimed Mom's fluffy slippers as their mother hen substitute – even when she was wearing them. She learned to adopt a sort of sliding action whilst walking.'


### ▣ HAPPY DAYS ON THE FARM ▣

'As a child during the 1920s and 1930s some of my happiest days were spent on my uncle's farm where I learnt to hand milk the cows, muck out the pigsty and at lambing time bottle feed any orphan lambs. There were hens to feed and eggs to collect.

In hay time we rode the cart horses or hay carts from the fields to the rickyard where the hay was stacked with a sloping roof which would be thatched with straw to keep out the rain. My aunt would bring baskets of sandwiches, cakes and tea for the workers (it was thirsty work in those days). One day much to my mother's disgust my brother and I found the cider bottles; thinking it was lemonade we got quite tiddly and had to be put to bed to sleep it off.

School was about two miles walk away until my Dad arranged for the bus to alter to an earlier timetable so that we could be in school for 9 am. It was a walk back home, though mostly uphill. We used to dawdle sometimes, stopping to pick flowers or wild strawberries.

It was my job to collect the vicar's newspaper from the bus conductor and deliver it to the vicarage each morning. There was a blacksmith's forge in the village where I lived, situated near the bus stop so on cold winter mornings we would go into the forge, blow up the bellows and get lovely and warm.'

## ⊠ THE BAILIFF'S FAMILY ⊠

'At the beginning of this century my father was the bailifff at Mercote Hall, the weekend retreat of the Mitchell family (of Mitchells and Butlers). During the week my brother and I had the run of the grounds. My father used a pony with rubber boots to pull the lawn mower; other duties meant that he had to protect the pansy beds with an awning and stoke the boilers in the hot houses late at night.

The family at Berkswell Hall went to Scotland each summer; they had a private train which parked in the siding at Berkswell station, and was loaded with food for the journey. The remaining servants would clean the whole house in their absence.

In the years before the First World War my mother would walk to Hampton station and take the train to Birmingham. She would go to the Beehive to order material for working shirts, Sunday shirts and night shirts. When the bolts of material came they were collected from the station with the pony trap or float. Nellie Brown came from Four Oaks, pushing her sewing machine in an old pram. She stayed with us for a week, helping Mother to make up the shirts.

Father gave me a cade lamb, which lived as my pet for 16 years. She ruled the yard, watching all that went on and protesting if her gate was closed. At the slightest opportunity she would be in the barn after the feed, or in the house, playing up and down the stairs or eating Mother's geraniums in the windows. She always had a superb fleece. Once it weighed 11¾ lbs.

Father loved animals – once he walked from Rugby with an ex-army horse called Captain. When Captain injured a leg my father rigged a sling from an oak tree to support him.

My brother and I walked two miles across the fields to Berkswell school. There was no heating; the water supply was the village well, and the toilets were buckets in the yard. We ate our sandwiches in an open shed – whatever the weather. We had to do the mending for the headmaster's family – I was given the socks as I wasn't very nimble with a needle.'


## ◙ GROWING UP ◙

'I'm afraid I didn't set the world on fire during my teens in West Bromwich in the 1920s. We used to walk up and down the high street in the evenings, hoping to attract the attention of the boys. For some reason, they called it the "monkey run". I never "got off" as they put it, I was always too shy and rather timid.'

'I was the middle one of three sisters. The eldest had lovely long wavy hair and the youngest had tight corkscrew curls, but my hair was very straight so I always had it in plaits, except for special occasions when it would be wound up in rags overnight – but what lovely locks for such a short time the next day. At age 15 I was allowed to have my hair cut so it was plaited up, rubber bands were twisted at top and bottom of each plait and the hairdresser cut them off, tidying up the ends afterwards. How shorn I was for weeks, but I still have my plaits to this day.

When it had grown a bit I went back to the hairdresser for a perm! There at 9.30 am, I left at 2 pm. I was ushered into a cubicle, curtained round (no one should know you ever had your hair permed then) and it all began.

First it was washed and dried, then they began by rolling small strands spirally round what looked like metal pencils. This took ages and when completed each pencil was inserted into a metal tube which was attached to a large contraption by wires. When each was attached, the machine was plugged in and I was given a book to read. From time to time I would look up at this great volume of metal and wires, weighing somewhat heavily on my head, and at times small wisps of steam rose. I was quite certain my hair would come off with the rollers, and all this time no one came near me, shut in this enclosed cubicle and getting hotter every minute.

An hour later the hairdresser appeared and began unwinding it all. The resulting picture was a horror story, as my hair was a great mass of tight ringlets all over my head. It was then washed again and set in dinky curlers at the top and twists of hair curled and flattened to my head with a hair grip. Ensconced in a hair net I was then put under the hairdryer for a very long time – again with another book to read. A cup of tea emerged from nowhere, which was very welcome by now.

Finally the curlers and pins were taken out and the hairdresser began brushing it out, twisting and turning the hair with seemingly no thought to the head it was joined on to, until she was satisfied with her creation. I didn't know what to say as this strange person looking at me in the mirror was, by now, purple with the heat and surrounded by a mass of curls.

I crept out of the salon dreading meeting anyone I knew and looked in every shop window as I passed to see the effect of that long session. Needless to say, in a couple of days it rivalled my younger sister with her own corkscrew curls and I longed for my plaits again.

People in the 1990s don't know how lucky they are.'


▨  WINTER AND SUMMER  ▨

'I was born in 1929, the fifth child in a family of seven. We lived in a house in the country, which was a mile away from the nearest village (Catherine-de-Barnes), where we all went to school in the village church.

We started school between the age of three and four years. We

*An outing by car near Tidbury Green in 1949. The 1930s Standard 8 often broke down – 'It used to be fun, I thought, but Father was never pleased.'*

walked to school in all weathers; after heavy rain the ford we had to cross used to rise up above the footbridge making it impassable, then we had to walk to school via the canal tow path. In winter we often had to trudge through snow, arriving with frozen feet and fingers. The school was heated by a large open fire in the middle of one wall and a coke stove at the end of the room. The older you got the further back you sat, consequently your fingers never got warm.

In those days we seemed to have hot sunny summers, and although we never went on holiday or anything like that, we had fields to play in and woods where we played cowboys and indians and swung from a rope in the trees, like Tarzan.

In the spring we always knew where to find the first violets and primroses, and a little later on wild strawberries, and watercress from the brook. At the end of the summer we would search for mushrooms and every year we went blackberry picking.

In winter we would go out collecting wood for the fire, we never passed anything by. If someone had a delivery of coal and a few cobbles had been spilt, they were gathered up and taken home. Sometimes on our way home from school we found potatoes and swedes that had fallen from the farmer's cart. Once we found an old car tyre in the ditch, we rolled it home and Dad cut it up and mended our shoes with it, not very comfortable, but it served the purpose.'

## GAMES, TREATS AND CHORES

*We played in the street and our games ran in seasons, using little or no equipment. We had pleasure in small things, like the sweets bought with our Saturday penny or watching the local blacksmith at work.*

### ◾ DON'T PLAY IN THE HORSE ROAD ◾

'Don't play in the horse road; those were the words my mother always said when I went out to play with the other children of Deakins Road, Birmingham when I was a child. I have rather vague memories of the First World War; of queuing for rations, the sound of alarms and then the noise of the Zeppelin engines and of Mrs Hinks from next door shouting, "They're here, they're here."

After that life settled into some sort of regular series of activities as the seasons progressed. Comics played a large part in my life during the winter months and soon I could read enough to enjoy the antics of the characters in *Funny Wonder, Comic Cuts, The Rainbow, Chips*, and as I got older, the *Magnet, The Gem, The Rover* and *The Wizard*.

Hide and seek had an infinite number of variations but our street's version went something like this. Someone was chosen to be "on" and he stood at a base (a gate post or wall) and covered his eyes. After a short interval he shouted, "Ready?" If no one answered he shouted "Coming" and set off to seek his playmates. When he found someone he then shouted, "Hi-acky" and ran back to base. However, if his victim managed to get to base first then he was "on" again.

For whip and top the top was made to spin by winding some of the string of the whip around it and then with a quick movement the whip was drawn away whilst holding the point of the top to the ground. This sounds very difficult but it was soon mastered. Another way of starting was to wedge the point of the top into a crack in the paving stones and starting in much the same manner. Older children with strong fingers could hold the top upright, give it a spin between thumb and fingers and drop it onto the pavement already spinning.

Tip-cat was a dangerous game played by two, the object being to knock the "cat" the furthest. The cat was a piece of wood about eight inches long, sharpened at both ends. It was placed on the ground in line with the direction it was meant to go. The player lightly tapped the end of the cat with a club or stick which caused it to jump anything up to 30 inches off the ground. The player then swung the club at the cat with all his strength in order to attain a good length of flight. Many windows were broken as well as heads.

There were many games of marbles but I can only remember the following. Two players each took a turn to roll a marble at his opponent's marble. A hit meant that the striker took the opponent's marble and so on. This game was also played along the gutter between the granite setts which bordered the kerbstone. As this meant that the players were actually in the roadway it was a dangerous game to play and mothers were always calling to their boys to "come out of the horse road". Another game was played where the players tried to knock a marble out of a chalked circle by flicking their marble at it from between thumb and forefinger.

When we were very short of pocket money we would sometimes collect horse droppings with a bucket and shovel. Certain householders would always give twopence for a bucket of fresh manure.

At Christmas time certain charities, the *Birmingham Mail* Christmas Tree Fund was one of them, gave clothing and boots to poor children. The boys got huge heavy hobnailed boots which aroused my envy because when the wearer kicked the kerbstone or pavement they would strike a wonderful display of sparks.'

## ◈ Copper's Coming! ◈

'The games we played at Handsworth were hopscotch, skipping – sometimes with a rope right across the road as we only had the occasional horse and cart to contend with – tip-cat, whip and top, and rounders. The boys, of course, played football in the road, till someone shouted, "Copper's coming" when they all mysteriously disappeared till the policeman was out of sight. I can only presume that football was not allowed on public highways. I can never remember being bored during our month's holiday in August, there was always something to do, or the local park to go to, or the swimming baths. We did a lot of dressing up using coloured tissue paper which was very cheap and we also did a lot of play acting.

Nearly everyone had a Saturday penny and many happy hours were spent deciding what sweets to buy. A wonderful variety was available: raspberry drops, lemon drops, troche drops, chewing nuts etc, all at two ounces for a penny. All sorts of weird and wonderful liquorice items were available for a half-penny each. Cadbury's did ½d, 1d and 2d bars of chocolate, and it was all chocolate not surrounded with wrappings as it is today. Of course, there were gobstoppers at ½d each which changed colour as they got smaller.'


## ◈ Delights After School ◈

'I remember in 1929 walking two miles to St Margaret's church school at Great Barr – no school dinners. In winter we took a stew dinner in a stone Dundee marmalade jar with us and Mr Tench (headmaster) stood the jars in front of the open fire at school. Mrs Cooper, the lady teacher, turned them round occasionally so that by dinner time we had a hot dinner, eaten out of the jar.

On cattle market days (the market was held behind the old Scott Arms pub – where the shopping centre car park now stands) we rushed from school to "help" the farmers drive their newly bought animals home. The cows, pigs and sheep had to walk from the fields of the farmers selling them, to market, then walk to the fields of their new owners. No doubt, we were more nuisance than the most wayward sheep!

Another delight for us on summer evenings was to join Jimmy

*The Brownie troop at Ullenhall in the 1920s.*

Parkes the blacksmith – whose forge was where the present Horns of Queslett pub now stands. How we liked to see the cart horses shod or the huntsmen's horses shod ready for them to ride to hounds to chase the foxes. The Hunt met at St Margaret's church, came through St Margaret's Hospital woods over the Queslett Road, across the fields and sometimes on to Sutton Park. On these occasions we had to bring our own pet dogs indoors as they took a dim view of the foxhounds who often "lost their way" into our gardens and kitchens if we left the door open.'

### ▣ OUR LIBRARY ▣

'My local library was Broad Street in Coventry. I used to think it was some sort of stately home, with its flagged floor and the oak bench in the porch, which, on a bad day, the librarians would shout at us for going near.

The junior and adult libraries were totally separate, and I could only just reach the counter when I began going there. Gramp told me it was a Carnegie library, and there were lots of them all over the world. Part of our fun used to be running round and round the counter, into the adult section, to see how red the librarian would go with frustration at us!

In those days it was four books for two weeks, two non-fiction, yellow tickets, and two buff ones for fiction. I don't think I knew the difference. I did know, and worry when they were overdue though, and would at times ink over a fictitious date so that the book looked like it was being returned on time, but then it fooled nobody because the librarian could not find them in the dated box, and eventually I was warned about defacing the books!

Changing schools meant being on the same site as the library, so my books were never overdue, as by then I was a bookworm with an appetite for anything printed, but despite this I found the graduation from junior to adult books very difficult, shunning the adult side of the library till I was at least 14.

We did go in the adult side in our huddles though, and egg each other on about the pink wooden book, in the health section. It was a dummy *Childbirth without fear* (a misnomer, if ever I heard one) by Dr Dick Read. This block of pink wood simply said on its spine, that the book was kept under the counter and had to be specifically requested.

Sometimes we plucked up courage to put forward a representative to ask for this, being sure it contained pictures of nude men – I can't think why, for the life of me now, but we were always refused on the grounds that it was an adult book.

Happy days.'


## ⊠ OUR GANG ⊠

'There were always four of us, John, Fred, Bill and me. We were all about the same age – eight or nine. Of course, this is going back a fair bit; late 1920s I suppose.

We played together after school and during holiday times and most of our games went on in the lane where we all lived. The games we played varied with the seasons of the year and the order was strictly followed.

*An outing to 'The Reservoir', Aston (now Salford Park) in 1927, with the old thatched boat-house in the background.*

In spring we spent a lot of time bird nesting and we all had egg collections which were kept in cardboard boxes and packed in cotton wool. We never took more than one egg from each nest; the excitement of finding the nests and sometimes climbing to reach them was reward enough for all the bumps and scratches and the scoldings over torn clothes.

When we found nests of moorhens or plovers we left only one egg in each, the rest we took home and had them boiled for tea. They had a lovely nutty taste. Moorhens' nests were often difficult to get to, being built in reeds or in low branches out over ponds. This meant a wading job with an old spoon lashed to the end of a long stick. Plovers nested in fields on the ground and the parent bird would often run away from the nest pretending to have a broken wing, hoping that we would chase her.

Spring was also a time for bows and arrows. Bows were made from hazel wood and arrows from young willow shoots with flights made from cigarette cards. There was fierce competition, not only for accurate shooting (usually at a potato balanced on a gate post) but also for the greatest vertical height. This always led to an argument as it was not easy to see who had won.

In the summer months our games often ranged further afield, especially a game which was for some reason known as Leo. It was really a form of hide and seek in which one of us would set off over the fields and hide. The object was for the rest of us not only to find him but also to lay hands on him. The resulting chases lasted for hours and sometimes finished up over a mile from home.

Of course now and again we had a craze for cricket which was played in any field where the grass was fairly short. With the crude equipment to which we all contributed it is a wonder that the ball ever hit the stumps or for that matter that the bat ever hit the ball. These games usually ended with us being chased off for disturbing the cows, whose presence had usually left our pitch with a number of additional hazards.

But mainly we played in the lane. Hopscotch was popular for a time each summer, the squares being marked out on the road with a piece of broken slate. The puck was a flat stone of some sort, the constant kicking of which was very hard on our boots.

Any form of wheeled transport was highly prized. Until it eventually fell to pieces we had hours of fun with an old pram chassis. This we rode lying flat on the frame on a cushion of old sack bags, shooting down the sloping driveway from our cottage, out into the lane. By lifting and pulling on the left-hand spring and by digging in hard with the right-hand boot toe, we managed to turn our chariot and set off down the lane. The spot where we stopped was carefully marked and each of us in turn tried to go further. This seems today to be a highly perilous pastime, but you must remember that our lane, in those days, was only used by horses and carts. In fact it was such an event if a motor car came past that we stopped whatever we were doing to watch it go by.

We spent a fair amount of time fishing for sticklebacks in one of the local pits, using home-made rods and string with a bent pin on the end. The bait was worm and the tiny fish, having taken the bait, were so slow to let go that we were usually quick enough to grab them and drop them into a jam jar. We carried them home in triumph to empty them into a rainwater butt. Our mothers didn't care for this and the fish didn't care much for it either, for they were always dead in a few days.

Saturday evenings in the summer were special. We all met on the godcake at the crossroads under the wooden signpost waiting for the fish and chip van to come. An enterprising Coventry couple (Mr and Mrs Mayo, I think) toured the district in a tall specially converted van whose arrival was heralded by the ringing of a bell, like those on an old fashioned fire engine.

When it pulled up by us the side of the van was lowered, letting out a mouth-watering waft of the delicious smell of frying fish and chips. We all managed by one means or another to produce a penny for a packet of chips (wrapped in newspaper, of course) but only rarely by clubbing together were we able to raise enough for a three-penny piece of fish. Salt and vinegar were free and never did chips taste so good and we cleared up the last scrap, finishing up by licking the last trace of fat from the paper.

We had all of us got bicycles of one sort or another, one or two even had rubber tyres which could be blown up sometimes and some had proper saddles; the one thing they all had in common was a lack of brakes.

In the autumn it was the season for cycle polo. Played in the lane it was a fast, furious and noisy game, the ball being hit with any sort of stick available. Spills and collisions were frequent as were pauses to straighten handlebars and bent pedal cranks.

At this time of the year, carts loaded with turnips or swedes passed up and down the lane and, following behind, out of view of the carter, it was often possible to arrange for one to fall over the backboard. Wiped more or less clean on the roadside grass, thin slices, cut with a pocket knife, were chewed with glee – swedes were best.

I remember once when a company of Warwickshire Yeomanry came into the parish on exercises causing great excitement. Some of them had white bands round their uniform caps to show that they were the "enemy". We lads followed them around, offering unsolicited advice as they stalked each other through woods and crawling along ditches. They had real guns!

On the Saturday of their visit they put on all sorts of demonstrations in the park (the local squire was their colonel), but the thing which took our eye was the tent pegging contest. A wooden tent peg was driven into the turf, and in turn the soldiers rode up at full gallop on their horses with lances lowered and attempted to spear the peg, lifting it up into the air in triumph. We were thrilled by this and for weeks afterwards we had our own tent pegging contests. Mounted on our bicycles and armed with poles which each had a nail with a sharpened point driven into the end, we tore round and round in Bill's dad's field, jabbing at a piece of wood knocked into the ground. In the end we got quite good at it.

The winter months brought very different games, mainly designed to keep warm. No grit or salt on the road then and any smooth and icy strip was quickly turned into a slide, each of us trying to extend its length. We all wore boots and it was widely held that a wearer of wellingtons would ruin the slide. Only one lad was ever allowed into our slide in wellies, and that was only because we found him useful. I'd better tell you about him.

He came from Birmingham and during school holidays he often came to stay with his aunt who lived up the lane. When he came to play with us it was easy to see that "townees" were a very different breed from us. He was neatly dressed and wore shoes or wellingtons. His hair was tidy and he was so clean – even his knees were clean and had no scabs like the rest of us and, incredibly, he wore kid gloves!

As I say, we let him join our games mainly because we found him useful. A ball kicked into a neighbour's garden would always be handed back to him because "he was such a nice little boy". We really treated him very badly and yet he kept coming back for more. Knowing nothing of country matters he believed everything we told him about the nesting habits of birds, the ferocity of bulls which were, in fact, only a field full of bullocks, and the existence of a very rare bird

which only nested in the thickest clumps of stinging nettles and whose eggs were worth a fortune.

Our favourite sliding place was on a local pit where a sloping bank gave a good run up to the slide. When there was some doubt as to whether the ice would "bear", we used to give the "townee" the honour of having the first go. If he arrived safely on the opposite bank, we knew that the ice was thick enough. More than once he waded out with wellies full of cold, muddy water, but despite our rotten treatment he kept coming back for more.

I suppose he must have been determined to become one of our gang and I'm sure he was disappointed when his mother put a stop to his visits from which he always returned looking pretty battered. We missed him.

How things have changed over the last 65 years. The lane, our playground, is now much wider and is always busy with fast moving cars and lorries and it is dangerous to cross from one side to the other. Apart from this, there are now no children in the area as most of the cottages have been bought up by retired couples or by those nearing retirement whose families have grown up and left home. I suppose it is all part of progress of some sort, but I am glad that in my boyhood I was part of a more leisurely life where the most important decisions were when it was time to change from tip-cat to hopscotch or from hoops to cycle polo.'

'Johnny was only seven when his father died and from then on the family finances were always on the brink of insolvency. There was nothing to spare for pocket money, so that it was up to him to earn it if he wanted money for the penny-crush at the cinema or a box of lead soldiers.

His first venture as an entrepreneur was collecting jam jars and wine bottles, for which the going rate was a penny per dozen. It was hard going as jam had to last the families for a long time in the impoverished district in which he lived, so empties were few and far between. They also had to be washed scrupulously clean before being acceptable to the rag and bone man. Wine bottles were very scarce and could only be obtained by having the cheek to ring the bell of the servants' quarters at the big houses in the more affluent districts of the city and asking, even then he was more likely to be greeted with a cuff round the ear or a few harsh words. However, by perseverance, Johnny could enter in his little notebook the addresses of places where he was more kindly received and bottles were forthcoming, sometimes accompanied by a slice of cake and a glass of milk. So successful were his efforts that eventually he was able to negotiate a better rate for bottles alone of a penny per dozen and was on his way to his first million.

The going was slow, but when he got to the ripe age of ten, he could then enter the coal-delivery business. This consisted of calling on houses in the immediate vicinity of his home and soliciting orders. The price of a hundredweight of Best Cannock was one shilling delivered, elevenpence collected. So having secured the order from the good lady of the house, it was hot foot to Chatwin's coal wharf to borrow one of their barrows, have a hundredweight of coal carefully weighed out and tipped into it and pay up the elevenpence. Johnny was not a very big lad, but was wiry and provided someone would help with an initial push, found no great difficulty in keeping the barrow and load moving until he reached his destination. Occasionally he got stuck, particularly in snow or on wet days when his feet slipped, but people were very kind in those days and never could he remember being stuck with no one to come forward and lend a helping hand.

Arriving at his customer it would then be necessary to raise the grating to the coal cellar, tip in the coal and above all, carefully sweep the pavement surrounding. Only when this was done to the householder's satisfaction would he receive his shilling payment. One whole penny profit, or almost 10% – not that calculations of that nature interested Johnny – he was keener on getting back as soon as possible to continue with his business. On a good Saturday morning, he could manage at least 20 deliveries, that is to say a ton of coal bought, delivered and sold and above all a very profitable morning's work. And as this became a regular practice, old Mr Chatwin noticed and was so pleased that he would offer Johnny the job of greasing the barrow axles after the morning's work for an extra sixpence.

Although Johnny lived in the heart of the city, he ventured often to the country at the appropriate time of the year in search of blackberries. He knew of one location where they grew in abundance, but unfortunately the local boys resented anyone poaching on their preserves. As it happened however, Johnny had a grandmother who lived on the way and owned a dog called Bob. Bob was a great pal of Johnny and as Granny was too old to take him for walks, his tail would almost wag itself off when he saw his young friend. So Johnny would collect Bob, who looked quite fierce being a Heinz mixture of bull terrier and another 56 varieties, knowing full well that the local gangs would give him a wide berth in such company.

It was on one of those forays that Johnny made one of his greatest discoveries – a small stream not only teeming with sticklebacks and minnows, but with an abundance of freshwater crayfish. A rare find indeed. Johnny soon found out how to catch them – a piece of string with a bent pin fastened on the end and a fat juicy worm. Dangled in the water near the bank the crayfish would venture from their holes, seize the worm and not let go until they were rapped smartly to drop into a Sharps toffee tin, the standard equipment of the time for carrying fish. They would command at least half-a-crown at the high-class fishmonger to whom Johnny would deliver them at the end of the day.

Then off to the canal which ran near to the stream and which was alive with water-rats. Bob was an excellent swimmer and rats were his natural prey. All Johnny need do was sit on the bank and let Bob chase and catch the rats, even in the water. Bob would return with a rat clenched between his teeth, already dead with its back broken by the strong jaws. The rats' tails would then be cut off and taken to the farmer whose land adjoined the canal and whose hen roosts and the eggs therein suffered from the depredations of the rats. A penny for each tail and perhaps an egg or two, or a bag of apples, and for Bob – sometimes a nice juicy bone.'

# SCHOOLDAYS: THE BEST YEARS OF OUR LIVES?

*Long walks to school, coal fires in the classroom, wet clothes steaming on the fireguard, strict discipline and liberal use of the cane – memories for generations of West Midlands schoolchildren, yet many of us have good cause to thank those hardworking and under-equipped teachers of our youth.*

## BERKSWELL SCHOOL IN 1907

'The infants played with sand-trays and plasticine. The juniors used slates and pencils, and did mat weaving with coloured papers – we adored our teacher, Miss Pollard.

In the infants' room there was an open fire, with a big guard, on which the teacher dried our wet clothes. When we were too cold to listen or hold our pencils, we were taken for a run up and down Lavender Hall Lane.

We ate our dinner under the shed – a long wooden bench with a tin roof and open front, and then played rounders in the playground. If thirsty, we took our enamel mug down to the well and dipped it in and drank heartily.

We wore long frocks, but always a white pinafore with plenty of frills and fastened down the back, buttoned-up boots, and gaiters in winter, galoshes for snow and very wet weather. Boys wore knee-length trousers with jackets, with a belt, and white collars.

We had many singing lessons with Mr Frewing and had a choir, which was entered for the Musical Festival at Leamington Town Hall. One year we came second, and another year we won the trophy (a shield on which our name was printed). Mr Frewing was delighted. The winning pieces were *Nymphs and shepherds* and *Where the bee sucks*.

On Monday morning I went with many more pupils to pay our mothers' Clothing Club money to Mrs Back at the rectory. At the end of the year my mother would go to Coventry to "the Manchester" to buy clothing with the money.

Once a year we went to Berkswell Hall for a tea party, and after to the Reading Room for a magic lantern session – on going home we were given an orange. Mrs Feeney from the Moat invited the school to tea and games – it was lovely as this occurred in the summer.

After a big dinner party at the Hall, we were told we could fetch "dripping"; lovely soft, juicy dripping – it really was lovely. My brother went with the other boys – I was too frightened to go up to the back door at the Hall. Mrs Jackson was the housekeeper and Mr Winifrey the butler.

We often went into the churchyard and sat on the graves and read the inscriptions whilst eating our sandwiches, calling at the well for a drink on return, and maybe peeping through the low windows into the crypt to see if the coffins were all safe and well.

We played rounders in the playground and if our ball went into the "private school grounds" (next door) they wouldn't return it, but we used to ask Mrs Callow to get it for us as she looked after the private school.

Mrs Bonser kept a little shop just opposite the school. Things were a wee bit cheaper than at the big shop – especially "Kali" and nougat.'

## ◈ CHAPPED KNEES ◈

'When I was a child the winters seemed very long and hard and I had to walk nearly two miles to school along country roads when I was only five years old. My knees used to get very chapped although I wore gaiters. When I got home my mother used to rub them with "Melrose" which was quite painful. I often had to go with one of my brothers to fetch the milk in a can from the farm after we got home from school. As it was then pitch dark I was very frightened.

How I looked forward to the long summer days and holidays from school. I would go over the fields with my friend Milly and take an old basket to pick dandelions for our mothers to make "pop". We couldn't wait for it to be ready to drink as it was so refreshing.'

## ◈ TURNING THE HEEL ◈

'When I was eight years old, I had mastered the art of knitting and the dishcloth made at school was passable. One day we were given four very pointed steel needles and some white wool, by no means the soft variety. The teacher, kind but very strict and no nonsense, proceeded to show the class how to cast on, using four needles, to hopefully make a pair of socks. After trial and error, and sore finger ends, I felt I would never get the knitting started. I saw the socks around growing and wished that I could get to the little bit of straight on two needles. That I was sure I could do well. What an achievement when I

*Barrs Hill school uniform in 1926.*

got to that stage. My poor sock by then was a very grubby greyish colour. Very soon I felt that I would turn the heel. Sadly it was not the case as I was making stitches all over the sides of my little piece of good straight knitting and the teacher was not pleased.

I was sent to the headmistress, a large person dressed in black who seemed to have the ability to see everything. She took my knitting and said, "What is *this* my girl?" A very weak reply, "My sock, Miss Thompson." She was not amused and I can't recall what else she said but she grabbed my arm, rolled up my sleeve and gave me two awful smacks. I felt so embarrassed as I returned to the class and I just wanted to hide away. Would that heel ever turn?

My mother knitted socks so quickly that she could not go slowly to show me. However, a very kind neighbour took me in hand. How I loved those knitting sessions with Mrs Patty (as I called her). She very patiently showed me how to cast on, knit carefully from one needle to the next and divide the stitches for the heel. At long last I learned how to turn the heel. I think the school socks were eventually finished and at that early age I learned an important lesson. The smack was humiliating but even now I try not to let anything beat me.'

### ❖ DURING THE GENERAL STRIKE ❖

'I was a pupil at Dudley Girls High School in 1926, the year of the General Strike and was asked to write an article for the school magazine on how the school was affected by the strike. This is what I wrote:

"I have come to the conclusion that the title of this account is incorrect, rather I think it ought to be 'How the strike did *not* affect the school', for like everybody else we managed to 'carry on'.

On that memorable morning of the third of May practically every DGHS girl set out for school determined to reach there somehow or sometime. Girls who came from a distance found many obliging people in cars, who gave them a lift on their way to school, while the poor town girls still had to walk in the ordinary manner.

It was surprising how, on the whole, girls managed to be punctual, and the school routine was little interrupted. It is true that every spare minute was spent in discussing the all-important question – was the miner or the owner of the mines in the right? – but no satisfactory decision was ever reached.

In the afternoon we were all summoned to the hall. It was announced that as many girls had long distances to go, school would terminate at three o'clock, which announcement filled the hearts of many with joy.

Next day the strike still continued and girls were helped on their way to school, sometimes by rattling in an old Ford van or at other times reclining at ease in a luxurious car.

At twenty past three the school was assembled in the hall and lined up under notices which bore the name of their district, such as Tipton or Brierley Hill. Here they waited until cars or vans arrived to take them home. Each district was attended to in turn, those having the longest journey going first. Gradually the hall was emptied until only the town girls remained to go home at their leisure.

So affairs went on. The assembling in the hall became a daily occurrence and the labels on the walls a familiar sight, and mothers at home anxiously wondered if their small daughters had reached school in safety or had been whisked off by some 'undesirable character'. Some days there were many cars to take us home, while another day about two or three cars did yeoman service. At last one afternoon the news was brought that the General Strike was ended. Of course everybody felt relieved, but life suddenly seemed very

uninteresting – gone was the joy of riding to school in someone else's car, or of toiling up hills on ancient bicycles; gone was the joy of shortened school hours and home-work not done, because of one's late arrival home; gone were all these blessings of the strike and life became ordinary and prosaic once more."'

## ▨ SCHOOL RULES ▨

'Most children started school at five years of age and I almost immediately caught ringworm which was prevalent at that time. I had weekly treatment at a clinic in Great Charles Street, finally losing all my hair. I wore a mob-cap for school and was assured that my hair would grow again and be curly – it did but the curls only lasted for a short time.

I think the standard of education in the 1920s was good. The majority of children in Handsworth where I lived attended the local council schools (later called elementary schools) and by the time we left the infants we were well grounded in arithmetic, knew several tables, our writing was beginning to form and reading was well advanced.

School rules in the 1920s had to be obeyed and disobedience either meant the cane or hundreds of lines. I don't think caning caused any psychological problems, it just made us be a little bit more careful. We didn't have a uniform, but my headmaster insisted that every scholar went to school neat and tidy and with shining shoes even though there might be a hole in the sole. School boots were available for children whose parents were really poor, but the majority of parents were pleased to boast that their children didn't wear school boots. Pawn shops were freely used in this period, and it was well known that Sunday clothes were pawned on Monday and redeemed the following Saturday.

Our headmaster was very patriotic and Empire Day, May 24th, was celebrated with style. Any children in Guides, Scouts, Boys' or Girls' Life Brigade and any other organisation were allowed to wear their uniforms on that day. We assembled in the hall and had a short service followed by the singing of *Land of hope and glory*, followed by

*Jerusalem* and after a talk on our Empire we ended with the National Anthem whilst we all stood to attention.

November 11th was also observed by the whole school assembling at 10.30. A service, which included the hymn *O God our help in ages past* was followed by two minutes' silence at eleven o'clock. During this two minutes all work stopped in factories, traffic stopped and if people were out and about they stood still for two minutes. Maroons were sounded which could be clearly heard indicating the beginning and ending of the two minutes' silence.'

## ▣ KERESLEY VILLAGE SCHOOL ▣

'I have vivid memories of the old sandstone church school at Keresley. The ground floor was the caretaker's home, the village library room and the parish room. A small turret at the side of the building housed the circular stone steps which led to the cloakrooms and classrooms on the first floor. An outside iron staircase led directly to the headmaster's classroom. The bucket toilets were on the other side of

*The May crowning ceremony in 1934 outside Montgomery Street school, in Grace Road.*

the road – places to be avoided if at all possible! There were three classrooms, each leading into the next; two had coke tortoise stoves and the head's room had a large open fire. The walls were painted a sombre dark green and in winter they streamed with condensation.

The desks were attached to benches and, although made for two, were all tightly occupied by three children. If one of the three spoke, we all felt the whack of the head's cane across our backs. As I recall, the head seemed to teach with a cane in his hand, but I don't remember the other teachers every having one. A later pupil told me how the boys would steal the canes and push them through the cracks in the floorboards. The lessons were very formal and we were not allowed to speak, but we all mastered the three Rs.

There was a small playground with a minute school garden beyond, where the boys were taught the rudiments of gardening. If weather permitted, games and drill in formal lines were taken on the adjacent common. Eventually, I left the village school and attended the girls' secondary school in the city – a very scared rookie!'

### ◈ DEALING WITH BULLIES ◈

'One day in 1932 my brother Barry, aged six, was beaten up on the way home from school. The culprits were two boys and a girl. He arrived home with a bloody nose and shirt. Mother came up to the school the next day with my brother and the bloodied shirt, and complained to the headmistress. She immediately took the girl and the boys, my brother and mother into each classroom and explained to all the children what had happened. "This is what I do with bullies," she said and proceeded to cane all three of them on both hands in every class in the school.'

### ◈ SO POOR ◈

'I lived in Aston as a child in the 1930s. People who couldn't pay their rent in those days lost their house and had to move their possessions on a hand cart to wherever they could find shelter. They were so poor that at times they had to look for a penny ha'penny for milk for the baby and their children took turns wearing shoes to go to school. Yet our school had the highest eleven-plus passes in Birmingham.'

'1942 is the first date I can remember writing in my own exercise book which was a half sized one with a blue cover. We had to use every single line. No space was to be wasted because when the war was on it was very difficult to get paper and pencils and we never knew if there would be enough to go round.

We didn't move up a class according to our age but as we mastered certain things. In the infants' class we moved from table to table as we learnt our alphabet and numbers and so on until we could write reasonably well and say up to the five times table and then we moved on to Mrs Badham's class. I never remember Miss More being very cross. It was a different story in Mrs Badham's class. She was quite a disciplinarian. There were different forms of punishment for talking in class. You could be given lines to write out over and over again – I must not talk in class – 50 times or 100 times if you had been warned. Another punishment was to put your hands on your head and oh, they did ache after a while. Again, if you had already been warned about your behaviour you had to stand on the form with your hands on your head. This only happened to me once and I was so ashamed I vowed I would never deserve it again and as far as I can remember I had learnt my lesson. If you committed graver crimes the ruler was used to slap your hands in front of the class and for the worst offenders, usually the boys, the cane was used on their bare legs.

We had desks with the seat all in one with the table part, and having room for books on a shelf under the top. These desks were designed for two people. I had to share mine for some time with Brian. He was a very large boy and he was the envy of everyone because he had some annuals. Nowadays every child has annuals but in those days they were very hard to get. Brian kept his at school tucked into this shelf on our shared desk. I was large for my age too and life was very uncomfortable for the two of us squashed into this desk which we shared with the annuals. There was no room for our knees.

The boys all had to wear short trousers although they were rather long short trousers, as you will see from photographs of the time.

*Arms neatly folded for a school photograph at Tidbury Green in 1946.*

Almost everyone had hand-knitted pullovers or jumpers which were often made out of wool which had been ripped out of an old jumper and knitted up again. Skirts and trousers were also often home-made out of a grownup's skirt or coat. During the time I was in Mrs Badham's class, one of my brothers started school. He was three years younger than me and a bit of a terror. One day when the infants teacher was away sick two girls from the top class had to look after the infants. One of them came to fetch Mrs Badham who, shortly afterwards, came back with my brother, holding him by the scruff of his neck. He had a ball of wool in his hand which was still attached to his grey pullover which had only half a sleeve on one side. He had ripped it out and wound it up. That was an occasion when I wished that I hadn't got a younger brother.

The desks in top class were larger and had ink wells in the top right-hand corners with ink pots in them. As soon as our writing was good enough we were allowed to use a pen with a nib which we dipped in the ink before writing. I always found it very difficult to write a line without making blots and the nibs would easily twist and sometimes break. There were monitors to help in class. One of the jobs was to collect the ink pots out of the desks and wash them. This was a lovely job, watching the blue ink streaming down the sink as you ran the tap water into the ink pot. When they were clean the teacher would mix some blue powder with water in a jug and the ink pots would be filled and replaced in the desks.

Every so often the nurse would visit the school and we would all file into the staff room one at a time to have our heads examined for nits and our hands for scabies.'

# THE WORLD of WORK

# ON THE LAND

*Much of the area that would become the West Midlands was farm-land, and so many of us grew up in a rural world. The farming year affected us all, in those days when the power on the land still came from horses and haymaking and harvest brought everyone into the fields to help.*

## ▨ A SMALL FARM ▨

'When I was a child we lived on a small farm of about 25 acres. We had five or six cows, whose names included Topsy, Daisy and Butter-cup. There were some calves, one sow pig – her piglets were reared for pork and one was kept for bacon for the house – some hens and one horse, his name was Jack. He was so gentle and willing to do any job. He pulled the milk float on the milk round. He knew where each stop was in the street, and moved on when told. He would also pull the manure cart, and be hay carting in the summer.

My father milked the cows by hand into a bucket as he sat on a wooden stool. The milk was strained through a sieve into the milk churn. Then the churn with the milk in was put into a big wooden tub which was half full of cold water pumped from the well, to cool it down. The evening and morning milk was sold on the milk round at twopence a pint. The milk was taken on the round in the churn, and a two and a half gallon measure bucket, with a one pint measure and a half pint measure hanging on a bar inside. The milk was measured into the customer's own milk jug or can which was usually left out on the doorstep ready. All the buckets and churns were always washed in very hot soda water, then rinsed thoroughly with clean cold water.

The cow pens and pigsties were all cleaned out with a fork by hand, the manure put onto a wheelbarrow then tipped into a big heap in the field. In early spring it was loaded onto the cart with large manure forks by hand, taken into the fields and dragged off with a manure drag, put in smaller heaps to be spread over the fields with a fork another day.

About mid-May the cows were kept out of some fields so that the grass could grow to be made into hay. That meant the cows were short of grazing. So for about one hour a day, the cows were allowed out into the lanes, to graze the roadside verges. My mother or my brother and myself (we were only children), would stay with them to see that they did not wander too far. There were very few motor vehicles, so they were safe.

My uncle would come and cut the hay with his mower and two horses. As it dried we all helped to turn it with wooden hay rakes and forks. Hard work, which would soon blister your hands. If it rained on it, you would have to turn it many times to dry it again. When really dry, it was pitched onto the cart and brought home to be stacked in a hayrick, then thatched with straw to keep the wet out. In winter the hay was cut out of the rick with a huge hay knife, which was very sharp. It was cut out in large squares known as a flake. My father would carry it down the ladder and into the cow shed on his head and shoulder, to be divided amongst the cows.'

## ◙ MOVING ABOUT ◙

'I was born in Back Lane, Berkswell in 1914. My father was an insurance agent and my mother a cook. With the outbreak of war the collection of premiums became more and more difficult. Father gave up his work as an agent and started work on a farm.

The following years became very unsettled. We moved from one farm to another chiefly depending on the kind of farm work my father liked best. We lived in tied cottages and were obliged to leave when Father left work. Our furniture and belongings were removed on a cart, Father driving the horse.

Before starting school I had moved from Back Lane to Red Lane near Kenilworth and then to Chase Lane, Kenilworth. While living at Chase Lane on a farm my Father had to serve in the forces. He joined the Royal Warwickshire Regiment and my mother helped with the farm work until my small brother was born. We were often taken in the pram while Mother was busy in the fields or farm house.

When my Father was released from the forces we went to live at

*Bill Duffin thatching a rick at Meriden in 1949.*

Wappenbury. Life was much the same, Mother at the farmhouse making butter, pork pies and helping to cook and Father doing all kinds of farm work.

A little girl died and we all helped to line her grave with snowdrops and ivy. As a sign of mourning I wore a white dress with a big black sash and a big black bow in my hair.

By now I had reached school age, and the nearest school was at Hunningham. There was a short way of walking there by crossing the fields. One day after a thunderstorm the fields were flooded; a stream from the river Leam had overflowed. The boys, almost ready to leave school at 14, carried the younger children shoulder high until we reached dry land.

We were almost self-supporting, growing many vegetables, keeping hens and pigs. Most farm cottages had a pigsty and a large garden. A neighbour kept bees and provided us with honey. For extra shopping, like clothes or shoes, we relied on the farmer going to market at Leamington or Rugby.

It was hard work for both parents. The farm work included cutting and laying hedges, cleaning out ditches (what has happened to ditches?), ploughing and harvesting. Morning and evening animals had to be fed and watered. Cows were milked by hand, the pens swept out and washed down. Calves, like some babies, decided to be born in the middle of the night; this meant someone had to be on duty as "midwife".

Sometimes at milking time we were allowed to watch and walk around, tasting the black treacle which was part of the cows' feed mixed with hay, swedes or mangolds. If we got too near while Father was milking he would say, "Open your mouth" and he would squirt some warm milk at us!

One hot day after being in the hayfield from daybreak to dusk, Father came home and decided he had had enough and he was going to a farm where he had sole charge of horses.

At Meer End we settled at a larger farm. We had a good sized farm cottage, and Father was to be the waggoner in charge of horses, waggons and carts.

Of course this meant a new school for me. It was a long walk to Balsall Street, where a new school was almost completed. I passed the Plough Inn, which is now called Tipperary Inn. As there was very little traffic I felt quite safe, until one day as I was passing a farm, a flock of geese gave chase and the gander hung onto the back of my coat. Although I had grown up among all kinds of animals, this was something new and very frightening.

As the school was not quite finished my first classroom seemed like a very large hen pen, a temporary wooden building; the teachers were very kind and it was here I decided one day I would be a teacher.

All was going well until one day the farmer returned from market and was too intoxicated to stop his horse. They finished in the duck pond, farmer, horse and cart! Father was blamed for not training the horse to stop!

Once again we were moving, this time to Bradnocks Marsh. Here there was a two bedroomed cottage with a very large garden. At the end of the garden was a small brick building. This was divided into two compartments. One was large enough for two pigs, and one for our outside closet. At night we used chamber pots, commonly known as "guzunders", and a slop pail with a lid.

Ducks and hens were kept in pens surrounded by wire netting. They helped to use up kitchen scraps, especially potato and apple peelings. The pigs thrived on a small quantity of barley meal and small potatoes, "pig potatoes", which were grown amongst the main crop. They were boiled in their jackets and tasted quite good!

Rats were the worst enemy, stealing eggs and killing the ducklings. The pig pen was a warm comfortable home for them. A fox would sometimes scratch under the wire netting and get into the fowl pen. In the morning we would find a pen of headless hens and others too frightened to get off the perches.

There was plenty of manure for the garden which produced excellent flowers, fruit and vegetables, which were shown at local shows. Cards and rosettes won for good produce were pinned onto beams of a shed adjoining the house. For liquid manure sheep droppings were collected and put into an old copper which was filled with rain water from the rain butt. Fresh water from the well was too precious for the purpose.

Mother helped the farmer's wife to make bread, churn and make butter. We always had good food, home-cured bacon and ham, eggs from the hens and ducks. A can of milk was allowed free daily from the farm and a rabbit if and when Father liked to shoot one.'

## ▣ A FARM AT EARLSWOOD ▣

'I was brought up on a farm in Earlswood, which is about nine miles from the centre of Birmingham, from the 1930s, and oh, how it has all changed since then!

It was literally "all hands to the plough and everything else" and at a very early age we were expected to help in any way we could. Over nine years there were five of us children born, my grandmother always arriving when another baby was due. When I was very young my father would lift me up into the hay loft and I had to push the hay down into the mangers in front of the horses. I was in continual fear of slipping into the manger myself. When the job was completed I would slide down at the side of the stall and, in fear of being crushed, would run as quickly as I could past the quiet old horse, who was, by then, contentedly munching her hay. We had about six horses at a time – Flower, Metal, Bell, Prince and many others and often we had a foal as well. I recall one being born during a thunderstorm which was named Lightning and another was named Monty after Field Marshal Montgomery. My father trained the horses himself, putting a halter and a long rope on the young colts or fillies, talking quietly to them, stroking them and letting them prance about in the yard until they got used to a light harness and learned to walk sedately round in a circle as he stood in the centre.

The farm drainage was somewhat archaic with a large drain with a cover on it in the middle of the yard where the pipes converged. Besides the hens we always kept a few ducks which were hatched out each year by a broody hen. I remember how desperately worried the hen would get, squawking, flapping her wings and running up and down the side of the pond when her "chickens" first took to the water. It just wasn't done! But one day, the ducklings disappeared and were located by their quacking in the drain. I was the only one small enough to go down the drain and so my father dropped me down into the large chamber and I had to retrieve the errant ducklings and hand them up to him.

During the winter months the machinery all had to be maintained and repainted. I was allowed to paint the cart wheels bright orange – I wonder now, why that colour? It was always the same, just as the kitchen had to be green at the bottom and cream at the top with a straight black line dividing the two. It never varied but it gave one a sense of security and permanence. In our spare time we helped feed the orphaned lambs by bottle. I had one special pet and named him Frisky. I'd take him for a walk to the local post office.

The work was very hard in those days and the hours long. Father

119

would be up as early as four or five in the morning when it was hay-making time to cut the grass, then get the milking done ready for Mr Izod who came in a little yellow van to collect the milk to sell in Hall Green. Later, Father had one of the first TT herds in the area and our milk went to Fowlers Dairies in Sparkhill.

Many times we sat on the wooden drill behind the horse with Father and with the land girl, Mary, walking behind as the corn seed was methodically dripped onto the newly tilled earth below. The hay seed was sown using a fiddle. This was a red box which you hung over your shoulder and operated by a sort of bow which you drew across the box and a spray of seed was sent out as you walked slowly up and down the field.

Haymaking time and harvest were extra busy although as far back as I can remember we had machinery – ploughs, binders, mowing machine, drills, swath turner harrows and many more, all pulled by one, two or three horses, and eventually an elevator with an engine which took some of the hard work out of loading carts and building ricks. We all helped with all these tasks. My father's motto when we moaned about a job being too hard or too heavy was "There's no such word as can't" and so we struggled on and found a way. After harvest the threshing machine would arrive. It was a dirty, dusty job although now looked on with so much nostalgia. There was a lot of excitement as the rick became lower and the rats and mice it harboured tried to escape. We had many cats and always a collie or two and the terriers belonging to the extra helpers who were always needed so the rodents rarely escaped. I kept well out of the way and watched at a distance.

The sheep had to be inspected daily and treated if they'd been attacked by maggots. Not such a nice job was washing out with disinfectant the crawling sores that sometimes developed but it was satisfying as you knew you'd made the sheep more comfortable. They were also dipped regularly. This was quite an event and I always felt sorry for the poor bedraggled animals as they surfaced. Shearing was done partly by hand with large shears and partly with a clipping machine that was operated by turning a handle. Again that was a job I was given at times, rather tedious. I preferred to use the shears but wasn't much good at holding down a sheep and shearing so I was left to turn the handle.

At Christmas there always seemed to be a litter of pigs due and no sleep for my father and brothers. Each year the butcher would arrive to kill a pig. My brother always had "tummy ache" and couldn't go to school. I was always glad to go so that I wouldn't hear the terrified squeals of the poor victim. Then the work began in the kitchen. Our elderly neighbour would arrive to help Mother in the dairy; pork pies, chitterlings, scratchings, faggot and brawn were all prepared and the sides of bacon salted and hung and the hams boiled. A very busy time.'

# OTHER WAYS WE MADE A LIVING

*There were so many other ways we made our living that the following can only be a selection, but it takes us from traditional village craftsmen such as the wheelwright and the cobbler to those who worked in the thunder of the factory machines.*

### ▨ WHEELWRIGHT AND CARPENTER ▨

'My grandfather and great uncle Alfred were the village wheelwrights and carpenters at Keresley. The old workshop stood for many years after they had retired; work became scarce when the farms became mechanised. As children, my friends and I spent many hours playing among the fruit trees at the back of the old workshop. There were no expensive toys but imagination ran riot using old bricks and bits of broken crocks.

I can just remember the horse and trap which was used to take my family to the city before the advent of buses. Often, as I sat on a stool in front of the coal fire on a winter's day, my grandfather would tell me tales of his work. As well as the normal farm work, he and his brother would go to a cottage where someone had died. They measured the corpse and then returned to make the coffin. There were no

121

*High Street, Harborne in the 1920s, lined with small businesses.*

chapels of rest in those days and the dead remained in the house – children usually being farmed out to relatives or friends.

My last recollection of any work being done was when I was about five years old. The men had been busy making a huge wheel for a farm cart. A large iron hoop was placed on the ground in the workshop yard. It was then covered with huge piles of wood shavings. Paraffin was poured liberally over the shavings, the match applied, and the flames roared and crackled. We watched fascinated until the flames began to die down. With long-handled tongs, the men lifted the red-hot iron ring and placed it on the wooden wheel. It was quickly hammered into place and then buckets of water were thrown over the wheel, making clouds of steam hiss and splutter in the air.

Years ago the village was sometimes called the "soapsud village" because many of the women in the village earned very welcome extra money by doing the washing for the wealthy inhabitants of Coventry. There were also three large laundries employing village women – nothing like modern launderettes!'

### ◈ A CRAFTSMAN COBBLER ◈

'Grandad lived in a terraced house in Percy Road, Sparkhill. The room at the back of the house was his workshop, he was a real craftsman. He could rebuild boots and shoes until they looked like new.

At the end of Percy Road by the Warwick Road was a large shoe repair shop and if they had any serious repairs which they could not manage they would take them to Grandad. To watch him repair a pair of shoes was magic, he was such a craftsman.

When he was going to stitch a pair of shoes by hand he first had to prepare the thread, which consisted of getting the raw hemp and waxing it, and then putting a pig's bristle on the end for a needle. He needed two threads as he would pass one thread through the hole he had made with his awl one way and the other in the opposite direction so as to lock the stitch. Everything was done by hand. He had a small machine which he used if he did any repairs to the uppers.

When he was stripping a pair of shoes, if they had been repaired previously and brass brads had been used, he would save these and take them to the scrap yard.

While he was working, he would cut off a piece of black tobacco twist to chew. He also had beer in a quart bottle and he would keep having a swig out of the bottle at the same time as having a mouthful of nails, while nailing the soles on.

When finishing the shoes off he would sit in front of the fire so he could keep the irons hot to put the red ball on, which was a large piece of black or brown wax. At the same time he would spit into the fire and if he missed the fire, Gran used to go mad at him.

If ever he cut himself the first thing he did was put salt on the wound and rub it in. I never knew him to be ill, he lived to a good age but died during the Second World War.

After repairing a pair of boots or shoes he always put his mark on them so he could tell if he had repaired them before; the mark was four brads in the shape of a diamond.

I have seen him completely strip a pair of shoes, take the sole and heel off and put in a new inner sole and then put it all back together. Some of the leather he used was so tough that he used to soak it in water before cutting it.

He always said it was bad to wear rubber soles as it gave you bad eyes – I suppose it *was* bad for his business to wear rubber!'

## ⊞ GRANDMA'S OUTWORK ⊞

'My Grandma was widowed in her forties and left with five girls and one boy to bring up. As there was no widow's pension she had installed in her back kitchen a bench with shears and a vice. She produced hand-made scrubbing brushes, bass broom heads and what was known then as a companion brush, that was put in the hearth to brush the ashes into the ash pan. She did this outwork until her family were grown up and I remember when she was 80 years old she was still doing this hard job; her name was in the *Birmingham Mail* as one of the oldest employees.

She also did washing for several families at a shilling a big basket, finding soap powders, blue and starch, which was used then. I had to deliver the baskets and was told not to move off the step till I got the shilling. She lived to the ripe old age of 92 years and was never able to write or read, but knew if she was robbed!'

## ⊞ WORKING AT BOOTS THE CHEMIST ⊞

'Did your mother have an interview when you started work? Mine did. I'd applied to work for Boots the Chemist and had an interview

*Works outing by charabanc from RW Brett & Son, Birmingham in the early years of the century.*

with the Territorial General Manager, who gave me a small test on the lines of how much was 2.5% of £1, because this was the amount of discount given to doctors, dentists and nurses who shopped with the firm. If you couldn't work out that it was 6d, you didn't get tested any further. If you answered correctly your mother or father was invited to attend, so your background could be seen, as one had to be a young lady to have the honour of donning a white coat. Mother used to starch my coats so stiff that they'd stand up by themselves and I crackled when I walked!

If the day wasn't busy we spent the morning surrounded by large sacks containing starch and washing soda. This we weighed up, the starch into blue bags of 1lb and the soda into brown paper bags weighing 7lbs. Then we started on the soap, wiping the slabs of carbolic and brown Windsor.

We recycled even in those days. People would bring their own bottle to be filled with methylated spirits, malt vinegar or distilled water. As well as most medicines, glass was hard to find and things still in short supply after the war. Saccharin was a new word; we sold one packet for 6d or you could have three packets for 1s 4½d.

We weren't allowed to do nothing if no customers were about, dusting was the order of the day. The fixtures flanked the back of the counter and were made of mahogany, the top half backed with mirror glass, the bottom half a series of drawers with the Latin names of the drugs inscribed on them. Mahogany steps enabled us to reach the top shelves and it always seemed as if as soon as you got to the top a customer appeared. Woe betide you if he or she was kept waiting, the boss would appear at your elbow and haul you over the coals in no uncertain terms. The customer was always right; during the day you'd agree that it looked like rain, was very sunny, cold, hot or looked like snow, if your customer said so.

One day I was allowed in the dispensary and shown how to wrap up the medicine in a stiff white paper with the creases just so, and the ends sealed with red sealing wax. I was also entrusted to make pills; this was really hard work involving a pestle and mortar and much elbow grease. These pills were put into a red shiny box and labelled.

Nearly all the medicine was mixed on the spot. The ones containing addictive drugs had to be checked twice before being labelled "It is dangerous to exceed the stated dose", and put into blue bottles. These bottles had ribbed sides so one could tell by touch in the dark that they contained a poisonous substance.

You received some very odd requests during the day and people confided in you. One lady had me advising her what colour jiffy dye to buy for her vest, as it was to wear under her see-through nightie when her husband came home on leave!'


## ◙ BIRMINGHAM GENERAL HOSPITAL ◙

'The hospital stood bordered on all sides – Steelhouse Lane, Whittall Street, St Mary's Row, Loveday Street. Our Casualty Department in those days (1944) occupied the site in Whittall Street (which now houses the multi-storey car park). Opposite stood old cottages where our senior nursing sisters lived, surrounded by small properties hiding away small gunsmiths and other businesses, even to Madge's Tuck Shop just down from Steelhouse Lane opposite the nurses' home. The new nurses' home wasn't in existence then; cottages and a paper shop occupied the site. On the corner of Lench Street and Loveday Street stood Bethany House, which housed the other sisters, and the PTS, the Nurses' Training School which we entered for six weeks to undergo our initial training.

The upper floor of the hospital was undergoing repair work from the incendiary devices etc dropped during the earlier bombardings. During the height of the bombing, Lewis's basement had given refuge to our patients and operating theatres, as had Ashfurlong Hall, Jaffray and Burntwood Hospitals, when patients were well enough to be moved.

All departments in the hospital were run by sisters, including the kitchens, where sister happily stated she could feed her nurses on 2s 6d a week and I believe she did. Matron and her three assistant matrons and senior sisters were law. We were a large teaching hospital of 550 beds and under the guidance of the House Governor and his staff. We were in awe of everyone senior.

On the wards during the 9 am ward rounds trolleys had to be carried as did screens for the bedside – no curtains in those days. *No noise.* The patients were as regimented as the staff. All beds were made, patients washed or bathed (in bed) according to the seriousness of the case, then breakfasted. All spots on floors were polished away. Bathrooms, annexes and sterilizing rooms were all cleaned by junior nurses before the 9 am ward round. I can assure everyone, there wasn't a speck of dust to be found or a blind not at the right level or a sheet not turned down to the correct length or a bed wheel not in line.

Wednesday afternoons, when there was no visiting, the wards were turned out. Beds from one side of the ward were moved into the centre. Walls were then high dusted and washed. The floors were polished and bumped with the bumper. We always thought it good for our waistlines! During visiting times, Tuesday and Thursday afternoons 2 pm to 3.30 pm when patients didn't require our care, the cleaning of trolleys and cupboards took place – no nurses should be seen to be idle.

Off duty times were either three hours in the morning, three hours in the afternoon, or off duty at 4.30 pm for the very occasional evening off. We had to be in the nurses' home by 10 pm, reporting to one of the night sisters, or else you were hauled out and on the carpet the next morning – a visit to Matron. It was known on the odd occasion, and with prior arrangement with a friend whose bedroom was on the ground floor, to have a help up by a friendly policeman from Steelhouse Lane opposite. This didn't happen often – we were too tired usually and had a lot of studying to do in any spare time going. All lectures were taken in off duty time whether on day or night duty. One day off a month. Half a day a week. Salary £3 2s 6d a month.'

## ▧ A FAMILY FIRM ▧

'My grandfather was a Cockney, having been born within the sound of Bow Bells. He came to Birmingham to earn his living, his father having died. He had been articled as a solicitor but now had to help support his mother. Birmingham was expanding and he found work keeping the accounts of a small building firm. With his legal knowledge and business acumen, he soon became its director and by 1905, it became a limited company trading under his own name.

*Will Swift – 'Mr Will' at the family works in Deritend – on his wedding day in 1929.*

The "Works" were in Alcester Street, Deritend, not far from another small family firm run by the Holdens. Edith Holden later became well known for her nature paintings and walks round Solihull and as the author of *The Diary of an Edwardian Lady*. Holdens manufactured paint and both firms did business together.

In those days, sub-contractors were used only for very specialised work and the skills needed for building were all included at the Works. I can remember the large carpentry shop with the smell of wood. Workmen used to arrive with their own billy cans with a mixture of tea, milk and sugar, which was "mashed" with boiling water. The firm had its own petrol pump to fuel the lorries. They were yellow with the family name on the side; there was a screw behind the cab so that the lorry could tip up to empty its contents. On the first floor were the directors' offices; on the ground floor leading from the yard was the general office with the accountant and secretary. My grandfather was called the Governor and his two sons Mr Sam and Mr Will. They had to learn all the different skills of the trade before they could become directors.

During the recession in the 1930s, my grandfather, who was a Methodist, refused to build public houses but built the Methodist churches in Acocks Green, Solihull and Stourbridge. The firm also built schools – Wheelers Lane in Kings Heath and Four Dwellings in Quinton were two. During the Second World War, there was always work repairing bombed buildings.

In 1920, Birmingham wanted to start its own orchestra. The Town Hall was already famous – Mendelssohn's *Elijah* and Elgar's *Dream of Gerontius* had received their first performances there. Several city firms, including my grandfather's, contributed to the project; another donor was the proprietor of a shoe repair chain, and a great friend of my grandfather's, who set up a trust which still supports the arts in Birmingham.

In 1949, the family firm bought a comptometer, a machine which could add and do percentages, which helped speed up the preparation of tender documents as the secretaries could do the work which before had to be done by the accountant or the directors.

Safety at work was not given as high a priority as it is today, although the conscientious employer took care of his workmen. For instance, hard hats were not worn on building sites and asbestos was used liberally in building. I remember my father bringing home sheets of it which he sawed himself to put on the tennis court for our bonfire party. Having a tennis court at that time was a status symbol, I suppose in the way that a swimming pool would be now. My uncle also had one at his house in Swanshurst Lane.'

### 🔲 SALES AND WINDOWS 🔲

'It is just 45 years since I left art school with the intention of entering the display world; my ambition was to get taken on by a large department store and be involved in creating marvellous tableaux in their Christmas windows. This was at a time when windows were being repaired and new shops built after the war and the shop window was regarded as a little stage facing onto the street.

The smallish shop I first worked at had a smart frontage, with quite a long tiled entrance and a large window at the side of it. Only the resident window dresser was allowed into the window, me! Inside was a small screened off office for the manageress and a dark oak kiosk for the cashier. The rest of the staff were in very strict rank, four sales ladies, me and the junior and upstairs the lady who did complicated alterations.

Each Monday morning everybody had their own rail to attend to, round the sides of the shop. The clothes were removed from the rails, the chrome was polished, the shelves were dusted, and the shoulders of every garment were brushed. As stock came into the shop it was carefully ironed before it was put on the rails. It was then the job of the window dresser to change the display for the week. This could take anything from a day to a day and a half with the manageress breathing down my neck. The inside of the window was cleaned, I had to wear cloth slippers over my shoes so as not to mark the pale grey felt lining the window. Dresses and coats were put on chrome display stands, waists were nipped in, crumpled tissue paper was shoved in the bust and round the hips and when every crease and speck of dust had been removed a price ticket was carefully put on.

Meanwhile, in the shop, as customers came in the manageress called forth the sales girls in strict order; this was important as they were all on commission. So when the first customer came in the manageress called out, "Forward, first sales!", then second sales got the next customer, but as soon as first sales became free she got the next customer so the junior might not get a customer all day. I had to join in this when I was not busy with the window. In six months I earned about half-a-crown commission as I could never bring myself to tell the customers that they looked good in terrible garments. No customer was allowed to browse through the rails by herself; as soon as they stepped through the door they had an assistant at their elbow, swearing blind that the garment they were looking at was the right size, colour, length, etc. It was a hard sell. If the customer managed to walk out of the shop without making a purchase it was called a "swop" which was frowned upon. If one of the younger assistants was caught twisting a coat hanger in her hands she was shouted at as shop superstition meant this caused a "no sale".

In slack times we used to sit in one of the dressing rooms and do simple alterations. Customers who had paid five or six shillings to have an eight guinea coat shortened did not know that an inexperienced 18 year old was hacking inches off behind the scenes. For this I earned £2 10s for a 44 hour week.'

## ▣ BIRTHS, DEATHS AND MARRIAGES ▣

'I became interested in births, deaths and marriages when I joined the staff of Birmingham Register Office in 1947. At that time Family Allowances were just coming in and we were inundated with requests for copies of birth certificates. It was amazing how many people didn't know their children's birth dates. The record number of certificates we searched for and wrote out by hand in one day was 800. We finished at eight o'clock in the evening. We also, at that time, had a seasonal increase in deaths from flu etc, which meant staff had to be sent out to work with the Registrars of Births and Deaths as clerical assistants.

Later, when work became slack during the summer we re-indexed the old registers which was fascinating. We started with the registers for 1837 (the start of registration) and worked forward to the 1920s. The change in lifestyle and the way people moved around proved how little things changed up to the Industrial Revolution. The town of Birmingham then consisted of a relatively small area around St Martin's church. Aston area did not become part of Birmingham until 1912 and King's Norton (including Edgbaston) and Handsworth areas did not become part of the City until 1932. In fact, although I was born in Stechford I was registered at the Acocks Green office which was then part of King's Norton district in Worcestershire.

In 1947 Birmingham was divided into 16 local offices for the registration of births and deaths. Today all births, deaths and marriages are centralised at Head Office in Broad Street and copies of certificates are photocopied – no writer's cramp for the staff these days.

As a Deputy Registrar of Births, Deaths and Marriages I had some odd experiences. The first death I registered was a child of five whose father had murdered him. The father was hanged at Winson Green Prison and his death was registered by one of my colleagues. Thank heaven this would not happen today.

Over the last 40 years life expectancy has increased and infant deaths have decreased thanks to better health care and research into once fatal diseases.

Birth registration proved to be a happier side of my work – although one Christmas Eve I had a very drunk father in to register his son's birth. Today illegitimacy is not such a stigma and there are not so many adoptions. When I was registering more children were born at home – today this is rare.

Names always provided a great source of amusement. One man wanted to call his child "Windy" because his wife was so "windy" when she was pregnant. She was eventually registered as Wendy! There are always names that are fashionable. Heaven help the children named after film, TV or pop stars who will never be able to lie about their ages. We also had the girls who were named after the midwives who delivered them.

Until the Income Tax regulations changed, the last Saturday in the financial year was always a busy day for marriages. Staff were expected to be in the office by 7.30 am in order that the ceremonies could start at 8 am (the legal times for marriages are between sunrise and sunset – that is 8 am to 6 pm). We had as many as 169 marriages on one Saturday with the registrars working in shifts and six marriage rooms in use.

We also had to attend ceremonies in churches which were registered for marriages but did not have their own "authorised person" to carry out the legal ceremony. These are now few and far between. On one occasion I got delayed in the traffic and the bride drove round the block three times. I also acted as Registrar of Marriages for one of my school friends. She had the cheek to say afterwards that she didn't feel properly married!

We also had to take Notices of Marriage. The first one I ever took was for a man of 37 who married a woman of 70 – and this was in the days before "toy boys".

One of my lasting memories is being given the marriage register for St Giles' church, Sheldon to index. It had taken 100 years, from 1837, to complete the first 250 entries. The next 250 entries were completed in 15 years. It was a history of the area in one volume and also showed how quickly Birmingham spread.'


## ◧ ELMDON AIRPORT ◧

'As a child in Marston Green, the airport was always in the background of my life, and aeroplanes were of great interest. During the war, bombers were assembled at a factory on the present Elmdon Trading Estate (formerly Metropolitan Cammell) and trundled across a very wide bridge over the railway line. My father's Home Guard contingent had the great responsibility of defending this bridge – I believe they were armed with one rifle and a thermos flask.

In the years after the war, the airport was a venue for family visits to watch the planes. In those days, they had real names, not just numbers as now. The mainstay of the passenger fleet was the Dakota (Douglas DC3) which I believe is still used in some remote parts of the world. There was a flying school, using Tiger Moths and Austers, and when I was a Ranger I wangled a trip in a Tiger Moth and actually took the controls!

About that time, the RAF airfield at Castle Bromwich (now Castle Vale Estate) was still functioning, and I used to cycle there for the annual air show. We saw our first jet fighters – Vampires and Meteors

*Working on the roads near Tidbury Green in the 1930s.*

– and the V bombers, but I don't think they can have landed there as the runway was grass. The test pilots were the folk heroes of the time, we knew their names and read their autobiographies. And were told that they earned £1,000 a year! I'm sure they really did earn it, as aircraft design was pushing new frontiers and most developments weren't proven until in the air.

During school holidays I worked in the passenger buffet at Elmdon. Hard to imagine now, but there were seldom more than two arrivals in an hour, and the big event was the daily Viscount – an amazing 48 passengers all in one aircraft! We had some fun, between flights, as many of the porters were university students also doing holiday work.'


### ◈ OUR FLOWER SHOP ◈

'On 17th December 1934 my mother sat up in bed wiring sprigs of holly ready to be made up into holly wreaths. She had given birth to my brother the previous day; I was 15 months old and my parents had opened their flower shop the month before I was born. It had yet to make a profit and my father desperately needed my mother's help to get the business on a sound footing over the Christmas period.

The shop was just a rented lock-up and we lived a couple of miles away. My father had no car and went to market on the tram three or four mornings a week. What flowers he needed immediately he had to take back on the tram. The market driver delivered the remainder later in the day.

Dad opened the shop every day of the year, including Christmas morning for people buying flowers for the cemetery. His main trade was cut flowers and what he termed "making-up" – floral tributes for funerals and wedding flowers. I still have some of his old order books and they make fascinating reading. In the months before the war broke out, it seems that everyone who was "courting" decided to get married. On Saturday, 5th August 1939, my parents did the flowers for seven weddings (bridal bouquets 7s 6d, bridesmaids' bouquets 5s each, buttonholes 3d!). The order book also shows that the shop was open for people to collect flowers at 9.30 pm on Friday, 4th August, and at 7 am the next morning.

My mother can still remember sitting up all night making wreaths and floral designs for funerals at exceptionally busy times; everyone

used to send flowers in those days, donations to charity are apparently a recent practice.

The shop closed during the war, and afterwards life for my parents became a little easier. They bought a shop with living accommodation and Dad learned to drive and bought an estate car so he no longer had to rely on a kind friend to help out with deliveries.'


## ▦ PAWNBROKING ▦

'At the age of 14, on leaving school in 1927, I started my working life as a pawnbroker's assistant. My employer was William Edwin Holt of 140 Ladypool Road, Sparkbrook: "Pawnbroker, Jeweller and Furniture Dealer. Money lent on Cycles, Sewing Machines, Gold and Silver Plate, Clocks, Bronzes, Guns and every kind of Household Goods. Est: 1863. Successor to H. A. Holtom."

The Loan Office had a separate entrance from the main shop, which was large and double fronted. Apart from unredeemed pledges, we sold new goods, ranging from carpets and rugs to suitcases, umbrellas, mirrors, pictures and numerous household goods. At 8.30 am each Monday morning a queue would start to form outside the Loan Office, and from 9 am till lunch time we would work almost non-stop taking in pledges, which were mainly "Sunday best" clothes. As the school-leaver assistant, my job would be to stand at a desk, and enter into a huge ledger the name and address of the customer and the loan amount, and then write out the pawn ticket. I needed to be a fast writer and good speller, each ticket required a brief description of the article pledged and amount of the loan. After the morning rush, all pledges had to be taken into the stock room. Bundles were always in cloth wrappers, no paper-wrapped bundles were accepted, and stacked neatly with the counterfoil pawn ticket number pinned to the front, always in numerical order for easy finding when redeemed. Tuesdays, bundles mostly consisted of the clean washing the hard-up housewives had done the day before, and often the flat iron still warm from use, on which we would loan sevenpence. This most often was spent on stewing beef which cost 6d per pound at the nearby butcher's, enough to provide a family meal along with cheap vegetables bought from one of the many barrow-boys who lined Ladypool Road.

At the end of each month, the manageress would "open" unredeemed pledges; if not redeemed within one year, plus seven days, the pledge would become the property of the pawnbroker, unless renewed. Each article was priced and put up for sale. A gent's suit in good condition, on which we had perhaps loaned £1, would normally sell for 30 shillings; an old fashioned herring-bone twill sheet, on which we would lend, if in sound condition, one and ninepence, could sell for two and threepence. Even at that price, our hard-up customers would need to lay-it-by and pay in instalments. The end of the month was always a busy time, our regulars knowing it was "Bargain Time". We had a big, coffin-like wooden box, which I would place, or rather drag, just outside the shop door on which was written in white chalk, "All 3d each". It would contain the more worn items, such as towels, tea-cloths and underwear. It always attracted a small crowd.

Apart from soft goods, money was loaned on jewellery. Wedding rings were often pawned, which I knew gave a sense of shame to the customer, and we did a regular trade on selling rolled gold wedding rings, new for one shilling, always choosing one as near in shape and style to the genuine 22ct gold one. As soon as the rolled gold one discoloured, it would be discarded for a new one.

Friday nights were always hectic – as soon as the menfolk arrived home with their weekly wages, the housewives would redeem the best clothes to be worn during the weekend, and wedding rings worn again until Monday – then pawned again to pay the rent, etc. It was the cheapest method of borrowing money, one penny interest per month or part of a month on each two shilling loan, and one penny for the ticket, a slight increase in the cost, the higher the loan.'

### ▨ ON THE TELEPHONE EXCHANGE ▨

'Hampton-in-Arden manual telephone exchange was at 5 Bellevue Terrace from 1943 to 1946. The female caretaker operator was assisted by her son from 10 pm to 8.30 am when day staff took over.

The supervisor lived in Eastcote Lane. Full time staff were supplied by GPO Telephone House; the part-timer took over at 6 pm until 10 pm.

It was considered quite a feather in your cap if you were selected to be a relief operator; I was one of three. The other girls also went to Earlswood and Lapworth. The big incentive was travelling time expenses which were a shilling a day. We all managed to save on travel. For myself, I cycled from Birmingham to Hodge Hill during the summer. If the weather was bad then I took a "workman's return" from Stechford for Yardley station; cost 7½d daily before 8 am. I was also able to have lunch with my sister-in-law who lived in Station Road. Another saving! No canteen meals.

The regular staff were very friendly with some of the subscribers, but in the main we were operators and the general public were always right. There were some extremely rude people who treated the staff with contempt, but this was forgotten as so many were understanding.

It was a very busy exchange, the mornings in particular. That was when most bad tempers surfaced from having to wait. The outlets were very limited, from memory I think there were only five or six, incoming from Birmingham and outward for trunk calls. There were also lines where code numbers could be used for the Coventry area.

We worked a 48-hour week and in 1946 I was getting around £4 per week. Good money in those days.

The doctor in the area used to phone up and tell us when he went on an emergency, so that we could save people being upset when they got no reply.'


⊠ A PART OF FOLESHILL ⊠

'A smile from the stoker of the factory boiler allowed a four year old to enter the dark boiler house and hold out nervous hands towards the circular door of the boiler, which was open to allow the stoker to throw two or three shovels full of the silvery grey coke on to the fire. The fire was nearly at white heat and was a reminder of the hell-fire illustrations in the lurid pictures of Grandfather's Bible. But on a cold January day on the way home from school, it was very warming.

The boiler provided power to the 30 or 40 looms in the factory weaving elastic webbing. It also moved the shuttle in five workshops which were placed on the left-hand side along the short pudding-bag street. Between each workshop was a cottage with two ground floor rooms, a spiral stair reaching two small bedrooms. There was a sink in the corner of the workshop, a closet across the yard in the garden, a galvanised loose tin bath and no running water. For several years whilst my father was on the Somme and Mother helping to make shells for guns, I slept in one of the bedrooms and over my bed was the turning shafting making the looms work.

My grandparents were very proud of their faultless ribbons saying "HMS Dauntless" for sailors' cap badges.

On Friday morning the completed weaving for the week was carefully enfolded in a large red silky shawl, knotted, and Grandfather's stick pushed through the knot. He set off to walk to Much Park Street where stood the premises of Franklins, who collected the work of the out-weavers and added to their own output. Grandfather returned to Foleshill with silks for Mother to put on bobbins, with holed and patterned cards for the Jacquard looms and for my aunt to thread the right coloured silks through the innumerable holes, and Grandfather also brought back a few shillings for the work of the previous week.'

## THE CLARENDON STAMPING CO

'I started work at the Clarendon Stamping Co, Aston, Birmingham in 1935 in the assembly shop. We made brass fittings for coffins, cabinet handles and brass bedsteads. There was an agency in Africa for the brass bedsteads, they had to be of brass because the white ants destroyed wooden ones or they rotted. This agency was a very important part of our firm, and those orders kept us going through very hard times in the 1930s.

My pay was ten shillings per week, with a shilling rise each birthday. The firm was run by two cousins, Mr Gerald Parr and Mr Neville Parr. Each year when we were given our rise, Mr Gerald would say, "We could get a 14 year old to do this, you know."

*Assembly workers at the Clarendon Stamping Company in the late 1930s.*

Each week as we were paid we queued up in front of the account- ant who sat on a high stool at a sloping desk and the money was put into our hands. I gave Mother most of my wages – I only kept a shil- ling for myself. I could get a pair of stockings for 9d at Timpson Shoe Shop. Phyllis had a slightly better job – she was in the packing shop – but the pay was the same! In most places the pay was about the same – Hercules cycle factory only paid ten shillings per week at that time.

Mum worked for the same firm as me. She was in the press shop where the stems of the brass knobs had to be dipped in boiling lead. Standing over this molten lead Mum would often faint from the fumes. Mum's wages were 22 shillings for a 52 hour week. From Monday to Friday we worked from 8 am to 6 pm daily and from 8 am to 12 pm on Saturdays. We had one hour off at lunch time. There were no holidays, only bank holidays – Christmas, Easter and August, but, of course, there was no pay on those days.

We had no uniforms, we each provided our own overalls. There was a "Club" and we paid in a little each week. Once we had very fancy overalls with Egyptian pictures on them; we were the envy of all the other girls and had plenty of wolf whistles from the boys working in the factory.

When the firm changed from gas to electricity Doris, the smallest girl working in the factory, was sent to crawl through the rafters to install the electric wiring in the roof. She was the only one tiny enough to get into the space.

We were able to go home at lunch time as home was less than ten minutes walk away. We would prepare something before work in the morning, dash home, light the gas and cook the meal, eat it and dash back to work within the hour.

We had to clean our own work place and all the offices as well. We scrubbed the floors and polished them on our hands and knees.

The rent for our house was eleven shillings per week. When Mum was very ill and there was no wage coming in, I had help from the Hospital Saturday Fund and also Mr Gerald called me into his office and asked about my expenses. He made up Mother's money every week for years.'

## We Learnt to Lip-read

'I started work when I was 15. I had to take an apprenticeship for seven years. I trained as a weaver in the weaving sheds at Southalls. The noise was deafening and the first day I came home I had bells ringing in my ears. It was like this for about a week but you learnt to lip-read to understand what the rest of the girls were saying to you. There were six members of our family working there, it seemed to be part of our tradition. We made bandages for most of the hospitals in the country.'

## The Brush Factory

'The brush factory started in 1843, the natural evolution of a cottage industry. In the very early days "the old man" used to take his wooden brush backs out to the little houses in the heart of Birmingham and then collect them again, after they had been filled by hand with knots of pigs' bristle (a procedure similar to that used in the making of hooked woollen rugs). Collection and delivery was by means of a large wicker basket on wheels, which was pushed by hand from place to place. The finished goods, wrapped and boxed, were delivered to the wholesalers in the same way.

Then the premises in Highgate were purchased and rejoiced in the name of "Highgate Brush Works". This consisted of three or four houses on the corner of Emily Street and Dymoke Street. These were back to back, built round a square yard, reached by a tunnel between two of the houses, typical of the Industrial Revolution. For some 20 years these premises were used more or less as they stood. Fortunately they were not badly damaged by the Blitz, thanks to the diligent firewatching of several of the employees. My father found work there in 1919, after surviving the First World War.

When I first arrived on the scene as an employee, I was newly married and taken on as a "temp". Every Friday I managed to get lost whilst paying out the wages. The route was upstairs and down, out into the street, back into the courtyard and up an outside staircase, at which point I had to surrender and ask for help, when I would be ignominiously led back to the office by the foreman.

In 1958 the whole of the buildings became subject to a compulsory purchase order. I remember going out many times with my father seeking new premises, even as far afield as Alcester. However, these were finally found only a short distance away from what was to be later known as the "red light" district of Balsall Heath.

Feeling very modern, we entered the Swinging Sixties. Trade boomed, we exported to America and other parts of the world and extra staff were engaged, including me. Trade Fairs became regular events and I thoroughly enjoyed meeting people from all over the world, first at Earls Court and the Leather Goods Fair held at the Mount Royal Hotel in London and later at the International Gifts Fair when it came to the NEC.

There were the usual excitements that all factories have, like the time we had a knife fight in our yard between a girl's brother and boyfriend. However, there were the brighter moments too, such as the time when I opened the post and found a hair-brush badly in need of rebristling with the order form marked in red: "For HM The Queen". Those for the Duke of Edinburgh followed later.

In 1972 my father died and I, being the sole survivor, became Managing Director. At first we went on well enough, but the shadow of Far Eastern competition was looming and trade became increasingly difficult. After eleven more years and six months of acute worry, I sold out, feeling a traitor to my forbears. However, the purchaser only continued for twelve months and the property was on the market. Imagine my delight when I discovered that the final purpose of the old family business was to become an Evangelical church. Long may it continue.'


## ❖ THE MUSIC STORE ❖

'The music store in Birmingham was started about 1795 and then taken over by my husband's grandfather around 1900. At this time, the family were living in the house on Bristol Road, which in later years became Stanley House School and is now called Edgbaston College. The store sold pianos, instruments and vast quantities of sheet music. In the mid 1920s they were selling up to 100 pianos each week. Above the store were many practice studios, some capable of holding a 24 or 30 piece orchestra. Many well-known artistes came in and out, especially dance band people such as Jack Hylton and Jack Payne. In the 1930s a tied line to Keith Prowse in London was established, so the people of Birmingham were able to book their theatre seats direct.

However, pianos were very vulnerable in transit and had to be carried in slings, so the store owners formed their own transport company to Birmingham. Mostly they came from London, but many also came from Germany and the Continent. Later the transport company was so successful that it carried pianos for other music companies too.

Alongside the vast sales of sheet music since the inception of the company, the record business grew, until it had one of the largest record sales in Britain, taking the catalogue of many companies, ie stocking every record in every catalogue. During the 1920s another shop in the New Street Arcade was purchased, just for the sale of records.

During the Blitz the van store and the piano storage depot in Park Street were destroyed, as well as the shop in the arcade. New premises had to be found to back up the continuing trade in Corporation Street. They also needed space to house the service depot for radios which were now being sold. Some of the engineers employed there did war work as radio engineers for the government as well as experimental work with television prior to the setting up of the Sutton Coldfield transmitter.

Although the record department was still flourishing after the war – all new pianos were for export only – the older members of the family wished to retire, so in 1949 it was decided to sell the premises to another retailer, not in the radio business. These people traded for about ten years and then sold the site to Rackhams for redevelopment.'

## ⊠ FAMILY BUSINESSES ⊠

'I was born in 1919, at 46 Russell Road, Hall Green. My grandfather, William Halmshaw, was an organ builder by trade, who had a workshop with his brother at the beginning of Palmerston Road, Sparkhill. My father Joseph William Halmshaw was also in that firm of organ builders until his father died and his job came to an end in the 1920s. I can remember a Halmshaw Brothers plaque on the organ in St James the Great church, Shirley, in 1936. My father also worked as a carpenter when they were building the greyhound racing track in Hall Green about 1926. When the work came to an end he took a job in France

*Showell Green Cottage, Sparkhill, which had to be sold to pay off business debts in the 1930s.*

repairing church organs damaged in the First World War. After returning from France, he set up a workshop in Showell Green Lane, Sparkhill and made organ pipes. At that time we were living at Showell Green Cottage with my grandfather, Charles Henry Averill. He was my mother's father.

My mother's name before she married was Ada Eleanor Averill, and her father owned the firm C. H. Averill, Tanning Merchants of Vincent Parade, Balsall Heath, where the family worked in the business tanning and curing the animal hides in large vats ready for making into leather saddles and all kinds of straps and leather goods. About 1933, when the cars came on the roads, the business started to fail, and eventually went into liquidation and Showell Green Cottage, Grandpa's home, had to be sold to pay the debts. It had been a lovely home, with a dining room, drawing room, breakfast room, large hall and china room, kitchen and scullery, with six bedrooms and bathroom and lavatory. The bell-shaped windows in the front of the house with its bell-like roof ending with a weathercock made it very interesting.'


## ▓ TEACHING IN THE 1940s ▓

'I left the south of England for my first teaching post in the Midlands, in the village of Berkswell. Built in Victorian times and never altered the old school stood in the centre of the village. Painted throughout in a colour I always thought of as "baby-sick green" with its high vaulted ceilings and high windows glazed with frosted glass, the building, just after the Second World War, had a forlorn and forbidding appearance. The one thing I remember clearly on my first, and rather timorous visit, was a vase of vibrant scarlet dahlias standing on an old, and as it turned out, rickety table – they transformed the whole shabby room.

In one corner of the cavernous room that became my classroom stood a tortoise stove, an enclosed iron stove which had to be constantly fed with coke and which gave out heat and fumes in about equal quantities. On its top stood a large, fat, comfortable kettle ready to make that much needed cup of tea at the teacher's break time and also to make hot drinks for children at lunch time. Many of them had walked long distances in all weathers and had, perhaps, brought with them a little cocoa and sugar in a screw of newspaper, or an Oxo cube. A hot drink was some comfort in a harsh world.

There were two other classrooms besides mine. One with an open fire and a sky-light, which during the war had been broken by enemy action and repaired with a bit of spare glass from Coventry which had etched on it the amazing words "Bar Parlour". There was a cloakroom open to the elements on one side with three tiny wash basins and cold taps. The lavatories were just a row of buckets at the far end of the playground. It took me some time to discover why the girls were always so keen to fill the coke hods. Eventually I found out that they could run up the coke pile and look over the wall into the boys' open toilets. A source of endless fascination!

One of the most frequent visitors to the school was the district nurse, known as "Nitty Nora" or "the Bug Hunter"; she would look through the children's hair for lice and arrange treatment for those in need.

Many of the children at that time came from farms and tied cottages. I was always conscious of how hard the womenfolk worked to keep the children warm, clothed and well-fed. Not an easy thing to do with a large family on a farm worker's wage.

Much of my early teaching was with little boards and chalk. Now the school has been modernised, is beautifully painted, lighted and equipped and every child can use a computer, only the facade of the building remains the same.

After I had been teaching for some time and the school had grown a little, another, and even younger, teacher was appointed. The School Governors negotiated with the local landowner to allow us to rent an empty cottage in the village. Beehive Cottage, a little thatched property, was let to us at a joint rent of 15 shillings per week. We each had a bed and bedding given to us by our parents, the rest of our furniture comprised two old deck-chairs, a strip of stair-carpet and a wind-up gramophone. We rented an old electric cooker and a Burco boiler from the Electric Company at four shillings per item per quarter. We had a saucepan and a frying pan. The bath, left by the previous tenant, hung outside under the thatch and had to be dragged into the kitchen on bath night. The kitchen had an old shallow stone sink and a cold tap. Our toilet facility was a "large and small" scrubbed wooden seat over a bucket in a shed next to the pig-sty at the far end of the garden. When I moved into Beehive Cottage after living in "digs" – I thought I was in heaven! Each month, when we received our salaries, we bought something for the cottage, the sense of pleasure and achievement was almost overwhelming.

There were heart-stopping moments, of course, especially when our old neighbour would clean her chimney by pushing a paraffin rag up it and firing it. Lumps of burning soot would land on our thatch. We would be dashing in and out of the cottage to make sure all was well. We would hear her saying to her husband, as the flames roared out of the chimney pot, "Going nicely now, Dad, in't it?"

All this took place before it was common practice for young women to live independent lives. You either lived at home or in "digs". The idea of "those two young girls away from their mothers for the first time" (I had left home nine years before when I went to college) was a matter of great speculation amongst the village folk. If our light was on at what was considered to be a "late hour" the rector would be in school the next morning to say that someone had called at the rectory to tell him, and that we had better be careful. We led entirely blameless lives – we had to!'

# WAR & PEACE

B.E.T.

# THE GREAT WAR 1914–1918

*War came to the families of the West Midlands with the deadly flight of the Zeppelins and the march of soldiers' boots on the county's roads. Every town and village lost men during that dreadful conflict, and the peace celebrations were tempered by sorrow.*

### ◈ LIFE IN DUDLEY ◈

'I was six years old in 1914 when war was declared against Germany on August 4th. The family were holidaying at Bridlington in Yorkshire. My father took my sister and I for a trip in a fishing boat. As we passed another boat one fisherman called to the other, "Where are you going?" and the reply came, "Just sailing to meet the Germans."

*Queen Mary visiting a munitions factory at Coventry during the First World War.*

That reply proved to be, as far as I can remember, the only light-hearted remark during the four terrible years that were to follow.

As a child my life went on fairly normally. My father was on essential war work so was not called up. As the war dragged on food became scarcer, blackouts were introduced for fear of Zeppelin attacks. Zeppelin drill was introduced at school. I attended Dudley Girls High School which had a kindergarten and prep department so we were all involved in the exercise. The gym mistress ran through the school sounding a rattle at which sound we all had to leave our form rooms and file silently to the lower corridor where we stood with our backs to the window side of the corridor, so if the school was hit the glass from the blast would be blown over our heads! Fortunately, bombs were never dropped on Dudley and we rather regarded the exercise as a pleasant way to miss some lesson time.

In 1918 the civilian population was laid low by the terrible influenza epidemic which swept through the country and from which many people died and therefore it was felt expedient to close the school. As the staff had time to spare they, together with our enterprising headmistress, staged a performance of *Alice in Wonderland* to raise money for the war effort.

The school was actually closed when war came to an end on 11th November 1918. My mother and young sister had both been very ill with influenza and my elder sister and myself had to run the house and care for the invalids.

Here is a letter I wrote to my grandfather. He kept it and it was returned to me. I was now ten years old and it recalls how the news of the armistice reached our family in the days of no television or wireless. "Baby", by the way, mentioned in the letter was six years old:

"Do you know how we knew the war was over. Baby had been to the door to get the bread when she came running in to say the bread-man had said the war was over. Then we heard the hummers going and the church bells ringing, then we hoisted the flag and it did look gay. Daddy came home to dinner and in the afternoon we went into town, it was crowded and there were heaps of flags (I'm not exaggerating) flying all colours. Daddy kept saying 'Good afternoon' to people I did not know. Next day Mr Newy came across to see if we could

151

arrange to hang some flags from his window to ours, we did and it did look lovely, long bunting and everybody stared at it. I must stop now because of the washing up but I will write again soon."'

## ▨ FOOTSTEPS IN THE NIGHT ▨

'During the First World War when I was a young but observant child, the second in a family of five, Radford was truly a village. A long uphill walk separated us from the shops in Bishop Street where mothers went to queue for hours for butter (from the Maypole), and other scarce rations.

Bedtime in those disciplined days was strictly six o'clock in the winter and 6.30 in the summer which left long wakeful periods of listening for sounds from the remote world downstairs or the even remoter quiet, traffic-free road.

My very first recollection is not of sound but of sight, when I lay watching a light which swept backwards and forwards across the bedroom wall. The disquieting aspect was that a soldier in old-fashioned uniform moved in the beam and was staring at me. My

*The firm of RW Brett, Birmingham, used recycled cartridge cases 'salvaged from the battlefields'.*

elder (by one year) brother, when wakened, declared grumpily that he couldn't see any soldier, but the image has stayed clearly in my mind for nearly 80 years. Long afterwards I realized that a searchlight from the nearby Daimler aerodrome could have flashed across the room; but the soldier is still a mystery.

Even during the war, village customs were maintained and on a special Sunday in spring the stillness of early morning would be broken by footsteps and the chattering of people who had walked from the town to eat curds and whey from Warden's farm opposite: "Mothering Sunday, Curds and Whey, Palm Sunday, Easter Day".

In the tall sandstone wall of the farm was the famous Radford Spring which gushed endlessly into a low trough and then drained into Radford Brook. People came from quite far afield to collect the water as a remedy for sore eyes, and most families sent a child with a jug for the mid-day meal table.

One night there were hurried footsteps on the stairs and we were bundled into eiderdowns and taken downstairs for safety because a Zeppelin was passing overhead. The target could have been the Daimler works or the Ordnance factories at Foleshill. Subsequently three bombs were dropped harmlessly on Whitley Common where the craters could be seen for many years before houses covered the site. My father was away, so a neighbour came to carry us down, and on the whole we found it an entertaining interlude though the grown-ups must have been terrified. We had at that time special china candlesticks with curved hoods to shield the flame. These were called Zeppelin candlesticks.

Towards the end of the war, in the early summer mornings, we would hear the rhythmic tramp of feet but no chattering, only an occasional sharp word of command. The owners of these feet were the German prisoners of war marching from their camp to Radford Common where they were building Engleton Road and laying the foundations of houses to be built at the top of Dugdale Road. These houses were the first in Coventry to have electricity installed. The village children felt no animosity towards "the poor prisoners" and after school would go to watch the work and, with permission from the officer in charge, share with the workers their scarce sweets and try a little conversation. One young German seemed to gaze sorrowfully at my eldest brother, a blond six year old who perhaps reminded him of a little son of his own.

One starlit frosty Christmas Eve, probably in 1918, the Peace year, we heard many footsteps before suddenly a band right underneath our windows began to play "It came upon the midnight clear"! Why had the Salvation Army come out to Radford to play carols? Well, the bandleader, Mr Major was our next but one neighbour and he'd arranged this treat for a war-weary village.'

# THE SECOND WORLD WAR 1939–1945

*Once again, we were at war and the cities and towns of the West Midlands suffered terribly through days and nights of bombardment. Even small villages found life changed for ever.*

## ▨ WHEN THE CHANGES CAME ▨

'I lived in an area of Birmingham very close to the Castle Bromwich Aeroplane Factory (the CBAF to us locals). It was in these small and what would now appear to be very primitive buildings that our wonderful Spitfires were built. My eldest sister was directed into factory work and actually helped to build these aircraft, along with many other young girls, bearing in mind that the majority of young men were now in uniform.

Everyone was asked to give items of metal and most of the iron railings soon disappeared as part of the war effort to make weapons and aircraft.

And so, Sunday mornings would find people in streets and gardens looking up to watch the antics of the fearless young test pilot, Alec Henshaw, testing the Spitfires before they were handed over to the RAF. How we thrilled at the sight of our own personal air show and seeing these beautiful little planes being put through their paces – loop-the-loop, the victory roll, swooping so low we would close our eyes and then open them again in time to see the Spitfire climbing back up into the clouds.

Quite near to the CBAF was Fort Dunlop (where another of my sisters worked) and running very close was the canal. The enemy soon discovered that on a bright moonlit night (Bombers' Moon) they could follow the line of the canal water and drop their bombs either on Fort Dunlop or the CBAF.

To foil this, planks of wood were placed from side to side across the canal to cover the water. This simple device worked as the CBAF never suffered a direct hit. Had the factory been destroyed, history could well have been changed.

Later we had a US Army base in Castle Bromwich and if you were lucky, you would be given candy and chewing gum by these Americans. The arrival of these "Yankee" soldiers put fear into many a mother's heart and daughters were soon warned of the pitfalls of any association with them! The children were to be heard asking, "Got any gum, chum?"

Not everyone welcomed their presence, as the attraction of these handsome, well paid soldiers was somewhat of a threat to the local lads. "Over paid, over sexed and over here" was a common phrase directed at the Americans.

Eventually the war was over, the US Army personnel shipped home (some with wives and babies) and the CBAF closed. And so our locality got down to the rebuilding of houses which had been demolished during the many, seemingly continuous air raids which we suffered.'


## ▣ A DIRECT HIT ▣

'It was while we were eating our evening meal and talking about how great it was going to be tomorrow, when the Electric Department were coming to put the electricity into our house. A friend of the family, George, had been and done all the wiring and fitting of plugs and switches a few days before. Suddenly the sound of the siren and everyone started to move around quickly. I dashed upstairs to change into my old clothes and slippers and then out into our small garden (just big enough to take the air raid shelter) to help Mrs Nicholls, our

Issued by the Ministry of Information  in co-operation with the War Office and the Ministry of Home Security

# Beating the INVADER

## A MESSAGE FROM THE PRIME MINISTER

IF invasion comes, everyone—young or old, men and women—will be eager to play their part worthily. By far the greater part of the country will not be immediately involved. Even along our coasts, the greater part will remain unaffected. But where the enemy lands, or tries to land, there will be most violent fighting. Not only will there be the battles when the enemy tries to come ashore, but afterwards there will fall upon his lodgments very heavy British counter-attacks, and all the time the lodgments will be under the heaviest attack by British bombers. The fewer civilians or non-combatants in these areas, the better—apart from essential workers who must remain. So if you are advised by the authorities to leave the place where you live, it is your duty to go elsewhere when you are told to leave. When the attack begins, it will be too late to go; and, unless you receive definite instructions to move, your duty then will be to stay where you are. You will have to get into the safest place you can find, and stay there until the battle is over. For all of you then the order and the duty will be: " STAND FIRM ".

This also applies to people inland if any considerable number of parachutists or air-borne troops are landed in their neighbourhood. Above all, they must not cumber the roads. Like their fellow-countrymen on the coasts, they must " STAND FIRM ". The Home Guard, supported by strong mobile columns wherever the enemy's numbers require it, will immediately come to grips with the invaders, and there is little doubt will soon destroy them.

Throughout the rest of the country where there is no fighting going on and no close cannon fire or rifle fire can be heard, everyone will govern his conduct by the second great order and duty, namely, " CARRY ON ". It may easily be some weeks before the invader has been totally destroyed, that is to say, killed or captured to the last man who has landed on our shores. Meanwhile, all work must be continued to the utmost, and no time lost.

The following notes have been prepared to tell everyone in rather more detail what to do, and they should be carefully studied. Each man and woman should think out a clear plan of personal action in accordance with the general scheme.

*Winston S. Churchill*

## STAND FIRM

**1. What do I do if fighting breaks out in my neighbourhood?**

Keep indoors or in your shelter until the battle is over. If you can have a trench ready in your garden or field, so much the better. You may want to use it for protection if your house is damaged. But if you are at work, or if you have special orders, carry on as long as possible and only take cover when danger approaches. If you are on your way to work, finish your journey if you can.

If you see an enemy tank, or a few enemy soldiers, do not assume that the enemy are in control of the area. What you have seen may be a party sent on in advance, or stragglers from the main body who can easily be rounded up.

*'Stand Firm' and 'Carry On' summed up the government message.*

next door neighbour, who was in her late seventies and a very big lady, down into the shelter.

A little later all was quiet, so my mom and I went outside our shelter to chat to Mr Littler, an elderly retired gent who acted as our night watchman. After a few minutes the drone of German aircraft could be heard so we made a quick dive back into the shelter. We had just sat down when there was a terrific bang and we knew our houses had taken a direct hit.

Lots of noise outside as neighbours came to see if we were all right. I was first out of the shelter, stepping straight onto a feather bed with a loaf of bread and a box of Kraft Velveeta cheeses resting on the top. We were all unhurt but very shocked to find our houses down to the floor. We were the middle house of five and had been hit by an aerial torpedo. With the help of neighbours and my parents we got my grandma and Mrs Nicholls out of the shelter and across the road and into a neighbour's cellar for safety until morning.

At about 7 am I was all dressed up in clothes belonging to the daughter of the house where we were sheltering. I remember them so well. A yellow blouse, black skirt and a silver grey and lavender check jacket which were all two sizes too large for me. She was a big girl and they were her Sunday best clothes. The shoes were size five and I take a size three but remember, I had gone down into the shelter in old clothes and slippers. All dressed up, I went to see my boyfriend (who is now my husband) before he set out for work to tell him what had happened. It was his birthday that day, and we had tickets to go to the Hippodrome but I'm afraid we had not got much enthusiasm to go and we could not give the tickets away as no one else fancied a night out. It was the first big raid that Birmingham had had, 28th August 1940.

The fellows from the Electric Department did not have to dig a hole as Jerry had done it for them and we never did have electric in the house.'


### ▨ FROM BIRMINGHAM TO BERKSWELL ▨

'I can remember the air raids in Birmingham; going into the Anderson shelter following the air raid sirens. The bombs fell very close to

our house as they were trying to immobilise the train lines which ran at the bottom of our garden. During this time I had scarlet fever and Mom was issued with a red blanket to wrap round me in case I was a casualty – this was to identify me as an infectious case. If you were away from home when the sirens sounded there were large public shelters in which you went. I can remember one on the Alum Rock Road opposite the barracks. During air raids the ARP wardens would walk down the road and if there was even a chink of light coming out of your house they would tell you to put out the lights.

The shops and schools were bombed and I can remember seeing large slabs of butter in the grocer's window covered with broken glass. We also had to use someone's front room for school lessons when the school was bombed. We used to carry our gas masks with us and kept having to practise how to use them. There were very large ones for babies and they were put in completely. Fortunately we didn't have to use them.

After Dad went into the Army in 1940 it was decided that Mom and I would go and stay with my step great grandmother in Berkswell – she called us her evacuees. She was a widow and her three sisters lived with her; they took in paying guests who lived in wooden outhouses in the garden. These four ladies all seemed very old to me and they all wore long dark clothes and soft shoes and they "floated" round the house carrying either a candle or an oil lamp. We were allowed to live in the Garden Room which was an extension at the end of the house, mainly glass, and as we had no blackout curtains and the bombers were going over either to Birmingham or Coventry, we had to sit in the dark most evenings. Food was very short and as we only had one small fire on which to cook, Mom used one saucepan at a time and kept everything as hot as she could in a hay box. The only lights in the house were paraffin lamps and all the water was pumped and then filtered before we could drink it. One of the paying guests was a very big man and my mother was convinced he was a German spy as he used to flash a torch in the dark when the planes went over.'

## 🔹 ONE NIGHT 🔹

'I remember the air raid shelters being built in Birmingham. If you had a back garden at your home you were given an Anderson shelter with corrugated roof and sides which had to be dug into the garden. As we only had a backyard at home, we had to use the communal brick-built shelters at the bottom of our street.

After nearly a year of the "phoney war", the air raids began. Sometimes the warning siren sounded every night and so we got into the habit of finishing our tea at about six o'clock in the evening and then getting ready to spend the night in the shelter. Mom would get some blankets and pillows from our beds, two stools (for her and Dad to sit on), sandwiches, tea and a torch, and we would make our way down to the shelter where we met our neighbours from the street. The shelter had a wide row of steps leading down to the entrance at one end and an escape hatch with a ladder underneath at the other end. There was a chemical toilet behind a partition, and a few wooden bunks and benches dotted about. My brother slept in his wheelchair, other children like me slept on the concrete floor. We spent our time singing songs and sometimes hymns, playing cards and simple games until we fell asleep or the all clear sounded. Next day, my friends and I would go out to look for pieces of bomb shrapnel and would swap them with each other.

One particular night stands out in my memory. It was a Friday, near Christmas time. The siren went as usual so Mom, Dad (he was off duty that night) my brother and I set off for the shelter. We settled ourselves in and I remember someone gave me a slice of Christmas pudding from a white basin to eat. The local vicar came in to say prayers and to give us his blessing. Just then a crowd of people came

bursting into the shelter; they had been sheltering in a factory basement nearby which had been bombed and set on fire. Hardly had they
settled down with us when there was a loud whistling noise and an
enormous bang. Almost at once we saw green water gushing into the
shelter. We found out later that the canal near the shelter had been
bombed causing the water to flood down the steps.

There was a mad stampede to get out. Mom grabbed me, and Dad
picked my brother up in his arms, by now the water was waist high.
We struggled through and as we were going up the steps, I looked
back and saw the white basin bobbing about on the water. I remember us running along Newtown Row which was ablaze. I saw the
chapel where I went to Sunday school in ruins. The sky was raked
with searchlights, it was as light as day, and I saw aircraft overhead
and heard a rat-a-tat of bullets. As we dashed past the chemist's shop
I looked up and the whole front of the building was blown away.
Upstairs there was a brass bedstead and a pair of men's trousers
hanging on a knob, but there was no sign of life.

We reached New John Street and hammered on the door of a
house there. A lady let us in and we went down into her cellar, which
was full of people sheltering. I remember that I lay all night on a big
box full of empty jam jars, kept by the lady for jam making (you got
some extra sugar if you did this). Well, the all clear sounded about
five o'clock in the morning and we wearily made our way home.
There was debris everywhere, and smoke, fire hoses criss-crossed the
road as firemen still toiled on. What a relief when we reached Manchester Street, our house was still standing.

Later that day we went down to the shelter to look for our belongings. They were all strewn around on the waste ground above, ruined
by the dirty water. The firemen were there still clearing up, and we
were horrified to learn that in their panic to get out last night, the
parents of a little girl had left her behind. She had been found
drowned in the shelter, floating in a wicker chair.'


◈ EVERY DAY WAS A HAZARD ◈

'In 1942 when Britain was reeling under the blitz by the German Luftwaffe, I was working for my father as a clerk. He had inherited a

builder's and plumber's merchant's business from his father and it was situated between Dalton Street and Dale End in Birmingham. It was a very old building consisting of a narrow cobbled street from the old days that had been roofed over with glass.

In 1942 however, every day was a hazard getting to work from Stechford where we lived. The trams were very reliable but even they could not run if the tracks had been blown up or the tram wires were down. Most days we had to walk part of the way.

Every day new gaps appeared in the rows of houses or factories along the way and every day we were relieved to see Father's warehouse intact, but inevitably it became our turn and we had a phone call one morning from the warehouse manager to say incendiaries had fallen on the old buildings and everything had been destroyed except the brick-built part in Dale End.

Father set off to see the damage while Mother and I waited anxiously at home. He arrived home in the afternoon very down-hearted. Apparently the Fire Brigade had been on the scene very quickly but the water main had dried up and they just had to let it burn. A fireman told Father it was a very colourful fire with all the exploding paint tins! The sheets of glass had all melted down into most fantastic shapes too.

The only thing Father could salvage was the safe which was found intact under the debris. As we kept all our important books and papers in the safe we were hopeful we could retain some records of the business, but we had no key to the safe. A fireman told Father to try and pinpoint where we used to keep the key in my desk and then dig down in the debris and lo and behold there it was.

We had the safe taken home and the key still worked, and inside the books and papers were all intact but so brittle through being cooked they were extremely difficult to handle. However, with great care we managed to transfer all the records to new ledgers and day books.

The petty cash tin was also preserved. The coins were all fused to the bottom of the tin, and the notes were burned to a crisp but still distinguishable so happily the bank replaced them all for us.

By working from home Father and I gradually got the business going again and in time we established offices in the part of the building that had been left.'


## ◆ THE NOVEMBER BLITZ ◆

'I was never evacuated from Coventry. My parents said I was old enough to decide, for I was 14 when the Second World War broke out. I said if we died, we'd die together, although, oddly enough, I always knew I would come out of the war unscathed. On the night of the November Blitz, Mother, my sister and I were sitting under the stairs. The Germans seemed to begin with our end of the city. Early on we had a stick of landmines across our estate. Both front and back doors had been blown in and various windows broken. Father prowled around with a sand bucket looking for incendiaries and bits of shrapnel.

Our garden backed on to a first aid post. We heard the air raid warden coming up the road calling, "All cars for the hospital, all cars for the hospital." Father walked down to the front gate. We heard his voice, but not what he said. We heard the warden's reply, however, because it echoed down the road in the frosty air. "Thank God, I've found a man with guts." Yes, Father did have guts. he made three separate trips into the city centre to the Coventry and Warwickshire Hospital on the Stoney Stanton Road that night. Each time he had to take a different route because of blazing buildings, each time the hospital was bombed while he was there. On one trip when a soldier on duty tried to stop him, Father, so he told us later, wound the car window down and told the sentry where he, all his ancestors and all his descendants could take themselves to – he hadn't been an ex-sergeant major in the "Terriers" for nothing. In fact his language was so colourful that even his passengers, who were pretty ill, managed to raise a cheer. The sentry stood aside. Funny, I rarely heard my father swear!

Neither Father nor our car received a scratch and, strangely enough, next day we discovered our garage had had a great lump of brickwork through the roof, which, if the car had been in, would have badly damaged it. The next morning I shall never forget. We heard the all clear about six o'clock. It was very, very, faint and must have come from Kenilworth way.

**HOME OFFICE**

# THE PROTECTION
# OF YOUR HOME
# AGAINST AIR RAIDS

**READ THIS BOOK THROUGH
THEN
KEEP IT CAREFULLY**

*Every home owner made an effort to protect house and family during air raids.*

We had to leave our house – no water, electricity or gas, no doors, broken windows, half the roof gone and an unexploded landmine, caught by its parachute in the branches of a large tree at the bottom of the road, swaying gently in the morning breeze. I saw it. Mother and Father thought it might be better if she, Mary and I went to our friends in Herefordshire for a little while. Luckily we had enough petrol coupons for the journey. Father took a neighbour and her two little girls to Easenhall and managed, not without some difficulty, to get back to us. We packed what we could into the car, propped the front door to, and set off. Father drove along Kenpas Highway, avoiding an overturned corporation bus and many piles of rubble and abandoned cars, and turned left on to the Kenilworth Road at The Orange Grove.

By then, we were quite hardened to see hapless Polish, Dutch and French refugees fleeing from the Germans on the cinema newsreel. But these weren't *foreign* refugees, these were *our* people, fellow citizens, friends. They trudged along that beautiful road on that sunny,

frosty morning, away from Coventry. No fuss, certainly no panic, but slowly, wearily, a long continuous line on both sides of the road. They carried a few pitiful belongings. Families with cases and the dog on a piece of picture cord or clothes line, a bicycle with a case on the back and brown paper carriers hanging from the handlebars. Someone cuddled the cat, wrapped up in a blanket or shawl. A cat or small dog peeped fearfully out of the top of a partly zipped up shopping bag. People carried birds in cages. There were prams piled high with anything they could save pushed by mother, with father or sometimes the eldest son with a toddler on his shoulder and a case in his hand, whilst the eldest girl carried the baby. All of them plodding their way the five long miles to Kenilworth, or maybe beyond. Some may even have been killed five nights later when the landmine hit The Globe in Kenilworth. Who knows? Yes, it's a beautiful road from Coventry to Kenilworth, but I never drive along it without thinking of those poor souls, on the morning of 15th November 1940.'

### ◈ OLTON BOMBS ◈

'House building in our road ceased as soon as war was declared so the waste land was put to good use with the planting of vegetables in the "Dig for Victory" campaign. A hopeful council put out pig-bins into which we were supposed to put waste food, of which there was very little in those days. Two bombs, intended for the Rover factory in Lode Lane, fell on Olton, one in Ulverly Green Road and one on the canal bank opposite our back garden so our lovely new houses were badly damaged by the blast, along with the mains water supply. A tap was erected on the Warwick Road – a long way to carry a bucket of water.'

### ◈ THE WAR IN KNOWLE ◈

'I first came to the West Midlands about 1931. I was born in the Peterborough area, my father worked in the officers' mess at Wittering aerodrome. Because it was considered unsafe to have a small child on an aerodrome my parents moved to Barnack. When they decided to go back into domestic service I was taken to live with my mother's

*Land girls with Guiseppe and Melia, Italian prisoners of war. Prisoners were a familiar sight on the land.*

eldest sister who had an outdoor beer licence in Sparkbrook, Birmingham. Later she managed to get a tenancy under Mitchells and Butlers in Knowle, another outdoor selling also groceries etc. September 1938, the time of the Munich crisis, saw us on the move. We left Sparkbrook on the Monday – Birmingham's licensing day – and arrived in Knowle on the Tuesday – Solihull's licensing day. We stayed overnight with friends in Edgbaston. Travelling through Birmingham I saw charabancs on street corners collecting the Territorial Army members who were reporting to barracks and during the night we heard the rumble of army vehicles going along Portland Road.

The Tuesday evening saw us attending at the Wilson's Arms assembly room to have our gas masks tried on. Here I met our next door neighbour, Police Sergeant Ashby, for the first time. He had the unenviable task of coping with me. I hated the thing and felt suffocated until he tried a slightly larger size on, but I dreaded the thought of having to sit through a gas air raid wearing the mask. It was a time of great anxiety for everyone.

With the outbreak of war came many changes. At school one of our teachers left to join the RAF. All windows had to be blacked-out. The brewery supplied strong black material to all their tenants for this purpose, also a stirrup-pump to put out any fires – we never did manage to get it working. On our list we had about 100 registered customers, several families and some single people. Thursday afternoon was the time I had to weigh up rationed goods, butter and lard being delivered in bulk and margarine in half-pound blocks. As far as I can recall, the ration was one ounce of lard per person per week, two ounces butter, four ounces margarine, I think two ounces tea and about four ounces sugar. Single people came off worst and my aunt suggested they collect their rations fortnightly, they looked more that way. Other goods were purchased with "points" – tinned foods, biscuits etc – and sweets and chocolate had special coupons. These had to be counted each month and a return completed giving details of sales. Most months my aunt was summoned by the Food Office in Solihull to attend as the form was not correctly filled in. The end of the month gave her many headaches.

During the height of the Birmingham Blitz people would come out to Knowle every evening and spend the night, some in the Guildhouse or the Red Lion. We had about six regular visitors who also stayed with us over the Christmas Day as the buses were not going to run. The local baker, Mr Fred Curtis, let those who needed to, use the bakehouse ovens to cook their goose or large chicken if their own ovens were not large enough. Neighbours would come down our cellar when the sirens went, warning of an air raid, and during the day three classes of the schoolchildren did too, the remainder going down the stoke-hole at the church. We had evacuees from London, Birmingham and Coventry staying in the village.

Later in the war Knowle was really brought to life with the arrival of a unit of the Seventh Convalescent Hospital US Army. I was very nervous at the thought of what I imagined would be cigar smoking/gun toting gangster types. The only Americans we had seen were in films, and when three of these GIs walked up the path and into our shop I nearly passed out. However, they were only very young men, not much older than me, and very far from home and looking for a beer. My aunt took pity on them and allowed them to come in and have a drink. It was hopeless trying to explain the difference between Outdoor and Indoor premises and with the promise that they would behave themselves they were invited in. Thankfully everyone took a lenient view of this breach of regulations. That same evening these three returned with three more, they had between them three guitars and we all enjoyed a sing-song. The customers thought it was wonderful, especially when one GI passed round American cigarettes. We saw quite a lot of them during the short time they were in Knowle and got to know several, writing to their mothers. When they left practically all the village turned out to wave them off. It had been an education, meeting them, and a happy interlude during a difficult time.'

'One of my recollections of the war in Knowle is of Midland Red buses parked nose to tail along the whole length of Station Road at night to keep them safe from the bombing, ready for service the following morning.

I remember also the night Birmingham and Coventry received their worst raids. We stood at the top of our garden (some ten miles away from these cities) and saw them burning. The fires were so great that they lit up the sky. The following morning we had evacuees come to the village and they remained with us for some considerable time. Our little village school was so small that we all had part-time education, starting and finishing our school day at different times and we even had an extra weekly half-day off.

Through various youth organisations and our school we all contributed to the war effort in some way. I went potato picking at Johnson's Farm (oh, my aching back!) and was on duty on a local first aid post – we didn't have any casualties but we wound innumerable bandages! We knitted too – socks, gloves and balaclavas – and some very funny shapes they turned out to be but all were despatched to our forces.

The American soldiers were camped at Knowle – we thought Hollywood had arrived on our doorstep. They were fascinated with the village and its size. The local "picture house" caused great amusement but was much frequented by them. Of course, if it rained heavily it was difficult to hear the sound track with the rain beating down on the corrugated iron roof! The film often broke down but after a little while (and a few whistles) normal service was resumed.

Perhaps my fondest memory of the war is the Victory celebrations. In Knowle this was centred around our lovely parish church. We had been rehearsing the *Battle Hymn of the Republic*, "Mine eyes have seen the glory of the coming of the Lord", for weeks in preparation for this event. The church was overflowing with thankful villagers. The bells rang out for they had been silenced during the war, only to be rung to warn of an enemy invasion, and the church was floodlit – such brightness for our streets had been in complete darkness, devoid of street lights, and our houses totally controlled by blackout restrictions. There was sadness for some who had lost loved ones but the congregation sang with so much enthusiasm, I am sure our praises could be heard for miles around. A memory of such grateful thanks and joy and one which will ever be with me.'

## ❖ We Tried to Live Our Lives ❖

'We opened our home to a young couple from Sunderland. He had come to work at the colliery and we shared the air raids together. When they bombed Wallace Road the men went to help but there was nothing they could do, so quiet it was and terrible. We tried to live our lives but moved our beds downstairs. We spent our nights in terror under the stairs sitting on the gas meter not realising it was the worst place to be. We spent one night in the brick shelter the corporation built. It was so cold and we moved back home between raids. Dear Winnie was a great comfort to me. Her mother and father had come to live not far away. On the night of the big raid the bombs kept falling all night long and Winnie tried to dash out in the middle of it to get to her mother. We tried to reach her and her husband tackled her and brought her down just as all the slates came off the roof. What an escape. We woke up next morning; no gas, no light, so sorted out the primus stove to warm the baby's bottle. We moved about clearing the broken glass and debris then we loaded the pram and walked to my mother's.

My mother's house was already full with my aunt and cousins so we trudged on to Bedworth to Jim's mother's and her house was full with all her children and families so we sort of lived from hand to mouth and raid to raid until my aunt moved to Lancashire and we finished up on my mother's front room floor. Never was a big pram so handy for all our moving. I helped my mother, with her lodger, queuing up for food while she minded the boy, a joy to her. We queued for cigarettes and brawn and anything we could get, dashing from queue to queue, standing for hours until shops opened or the market men came, to get, perhaps, substandard stockings and how lovely, one day I got two tomatoes. Always used to finish up in the war-torn Lyons in Broadgate for a cup of tea.'

# LIFE WENT ON

*Despite the sleepless nights and the constant threat from the skies, life had to go on – there were weddings to be arranged, rations to collect and shortages to overcome.*

## ▨ LIFE IN COVENTRY ▨

'In the village we went to for safety there were several very large houses where the local lord (rather a famous one), squire and various titled people had withdrawn for the duration. If the villagers met them either walking or riding the men would doff their caps and the women bob and stand aside as these personages were treated in a most feudal manner. This was something that my mother and aunt, who had now joined us, could not give in to.

There were nights when planes would throb over the cottage on the way to Coventry and there was an agonising wait before news came through of family and friends still there. After 18 months my mother could stand it no longer and we rejoined my father in Coventry.

Back to Coventry where there were great gaps in the rows of houses and shops, piles of rubble, large concrete water tanks sunk into the ground on street corners ready for firefighting and the familiar city centre smashed, overlooked by the famous three spires and a forlorn market hall tower complete with clock. Any remaining shops had boarded-up windows with perhaps just a foot square of glass to show off their merchandise, the little they had. People queued for everything, travelling across the city for one item that they had heard rumoured was available.

With rationing housewives were registered with one grocer and a butcher. The food for a family of four for a week would easily go into a basket on the front of the grocer's bike, to be delivered at the end of the week. Bread and milk were delivered by horse and cart, the milk being measured out of a churn into a jug as there were no bottles. Our neighbour had four sacks on her garage door for people to put in their salvage, rubber, metal, glass and, I think, paper – it was collected by salvage men each week. There was little to go into dustbins apart from ashes which were sifted for any usable cinders. Coalhouses were empty, slack swept up to mix with cement to make "briquettes" to burn on the open grates. They spat hard bits of concrete into the room as they burned. There was still a blackout with no street lights and frequent electricity cuts.

One of my jobs was to collect vegetable peelings from friends and neighbours, these were boiled up to feed to our four hens – one could either have an occasional egg or hen food on the ration books. Our hens served us pretty well and any excess eggs were preserved in slimy, white isinglass for use in the winter.

Adult clothes were repaired frequently and then cut up for the children to wear. Sometimes parcels arrived from relatives in the USA, others went to the bottom of the Atlantic Ocean. They were so exciting with tins of strange foods like Spam, sweet corn, maple syrup and candies. Some included clothes which were immediately adapted for somebody to wear. Women's underwear was made from old parachutes, some pure silk, later from an amazing new fibre called nylon. Handkerchiefs and pillowslips were obtained from draughtsmen's old drawings; this was cotton based paper which when soaked and washed turned into a lovely soft, fine cotton material.'

## ◈ THE RATION BOOK BUS ◈

'The ration book bus ran on Tuesday and Friday all around the local villages to Coleshill, where the offices for any query on your ration book were situated. We used to catch this bus in Balsall Common, travelling through Barston to Knowle; it had to go on a roundabout route because of the decoy in the fields between Balsall Common and Temple Balsall, no one being allowed along that road unless their journey was really necessary. Lots of passengers got off in Knowle and caught the Midland Red bus to Solihull to do their shopping. Coming home we would show each other our treats, having had to queue for everything. A packet of crisps would last my brother and me a month.

With the building of Honiley aerodrome, the airmen brought new life to Balsall Common. Full trucks of Canadian boys became regular users of Berkswell station. Saturday night dances were run by a team of ladies, including my mother. They scrimped and saved and people gave so that there were refreshments each week. The RAF boys would provide chocolate and dried egg and anything else they could obtain from the Naafi.'

## ◈ SHORTAGES OVERCOME ◈

'We soon learned to stand in any queue that formed, whether for lipstick at the chemist or a bottle of sauce at the grocer's. We would soften the butter ration and then beat into it one of our precious eggs, which doubled the quantity and made it into an easy to spread paste. We came to like dried egg and many were the recipes swapped to make it palatable. All our sugar was kept for jam so the sugar bowl was banned from the table and none of the family has taken it since. Bacon rinds and other scraps of fat from the meat ration were rendered down and saved for pastry and the occasional fry up.'

'Potatoes and swedes were readily available at the farm and an occasional rabbit to eke out the meat and bacon ration – such a treat!

Clothing was purchased by coupons and "make do and mend"

became the order of the day. We had to be registered with a coal merchant too, thus making a walk along the hedgerows out "sticking" a pleasant way to keep the home fires burning.

It was amazing what we as a nation managed on. "Mrs Churchill's Downing Street Cake" was quite passable provided it was eaten fresh, as were "Mock Sausages" and "Angel Slices", to name but three. Chocolates, sweets and fruit were rarities, and the occasional jelly felt like a banquet!'

## ▣ GETTING WED ▣

'I was married during the war but in spite of the rationing and clothes coupons managed to have a white wedding and three bridesmaids – someone got the material for the dresses without coupons. We couldn't get a white iced cake so we finished up with a chocolate one with white decorations; I've never heard of anyone else who had a chocolate wedding cake. We went to a studio to have photos taken, and were only allowed one large photo of the bride and groom and six of each small photos of group and bride and groom. Someone managed to get a film and we had a few snaps.

On the morning of the wedding I walked through the park with my friend to fetch the flowers from the nursery and the man said they had trouble getting the roses to bloom; not surprising – it was Boxing Day in wartime. Then he gave me a great surprise; one pound of tomatoes. He said, "Give these to the bride with my compliments." I didn't let on it was me.

Back home panic was setting in as one of the bridesmaids was late. I finished up dressing her. We held the reception at home and Mother had done most of the preparing. One treat was the pressed tongue. It had been placed in a cake tin with a brick on the top to keep it firm.

When I look at the coloured photos and videos of weddings now, I think, ah well, I am still happily married after 50 years.'

## ▣ WARTIME DANCES ▣

'Coventry was fortunate in having many excellent ballrooms and during the war dancing was perhaps our chief entertainment. My favourite was Neale's Ballroom which attracted all the top bands of the day.

There I danced to Ted Heath, Edmundo Ros and the incomparable Geraldo who was so suave and sophisticated.

How we girls managed to conjure up long dresses in those days of clothes rationing was a miracle, but we always did. Unfortunately, we didn't arrive at the ball in style as Cinderella did, but rather stuffed our dance shoes in a bag, pinned up our long skirts under our coats and jumped on our bicycles, and the transformation took place when we arrived. If a suitable young man asked for the last waltz and offered to see us home we would allow him to do so, pushing the bike. After talking for a while at the gate and a goodnight kiss, for which permission was always asked, he would set off again for the walk home which was often at the other end of town. How times have changed.'

# DOING OUR BIT

*The Home Front provided many opportunities for everyone to do their bit for the war effort, from the women of the Land Army to the members of the Auxiliary Fire Service. Collecting scrap and donations, firewatching, canning fruit and vegetables – we all took on a share of the work.*

### ☒ MUM AND DAD ☒

'Dad had an allotment – a piece of waste ground to grow vegetables on. Everyone was encouraged to "dig for victory" and most people with small gardens had one. Our allotment was on open ground right near to the main Stratford Road, but I can't recall anything getting pinched in spite of all the shortages, and we grew some prize marrows and tomatoes! Twice a year Dad and I would go to a nearby farm and using the farmer's handcart we would load up with manure and trundle the truck along the Stratford Road to the allotment. I often think of those journeys when I drive along that very busy road today – what a long time ago it seems.

*A Birmingham Civil Defence Unit in 1940.*

My dad was too old for the Forces so he did his bit by joining the Special police, the younger regular policemen having been called up to the war. After work he would go to help man the police station or out on patrol. One night the police had heard that someone was stealing wooden fencing, so when Dad was out on patrol he saw a man pushing a handcart full of something that had been carefully covered with a tarpaulin. Dad stopped him to ask him what he had in his barrow and the man replied, "Pielins, sir." Dad, thinking the man had said "palings" and of the missing fencing, thought he had caught the culprit, so he made him take the tarpaulin off – the barrow was full of "peelings". The man had some pigs and he was taking them their dinner!

Mum was wonderful during the war. She would listen to the wireless and pick up all sorts of hints and tips. "Make do and mend" was a favourite slogan and clothes which were in short supply were handed down from cousin to cousin and altered to fit; sheets that had gone in the middle were slit in two and the unworn sides put to the middle. The sewing machine was in constant use. Food, too, was a nightmare – there were failures, I can remember her making carrot jam with very little sugar, none of us liked it but there was nothing else to do, it had to be eaten. Mother's classic remark came when Dad, bored with the food we were eating, moaned about having toast again and she said, "You think yourself lucky – some people only have bread"! Mother became a member of the Women's Voluntary Services (WVS for short). She gave her time absolutely free three afternoons a week to serve in a canteen in our local BSA (British Small Arms) factory. The war workers loved a cup of tea.'

### ◨ HOME FOR TWO HOURS ◨

'We moved to Tidbury Green at the beginning of the war. My father could not go to war because he was classed as disabled. He worked with metals for the aircraft at ICI. I never saw Father from one week to another. If he was not working on the furnaces he was guarding them from attack by enemy aircraft (bombs and incendiaries). If he was free then it was the Home Guard – he was a sergeant (with hand grenades and explosives).

If I did see him come home in the morning, he would have no shirt on as this had been splattered with hot metal which had burnt the shirt and stuck to the skin. He would be home for perhaps two hours then go back again to work.'

### ◨ IN THE AUXILIARY FIRE SERVICE ◨

'I joined the Auxiliary Fire Service in August 1938 and was called for full time service on 1st September 1939. I was first stationed at Cornocks Wood Yard on the common and then for a spell at Fashinos Biscuit Factory, and when Caines Garage was converted to a fire station, I was transferred there. Nothing exciting happened until the raids started in August 1940, then we had an incendiary fire in the cornfields at Shard End. I attended several fires in the city centre in October, but the real night of my career was in Coventry on 14th November 1940.

I arrived at Coventry boundary at eight o'clock, and was just approaching the gas works when they were hit. That was a good start. I eventually arrived at the fire station after a lot of diversion, and reported in. By that time the heavy raid was really starting. My first job was on a bus on the Pool Meadow car park. The incendiaries were dropped on a woodyard nearby, so I transferred to that. The next lot was dropped on the GEC factory next door to the cathedral. We were working well, when the petrol supplies ran out. I went to the fire station to get supplies, but was informed that the petrol pump had been hit. I collected a van and a local fireman, went round the pumps at work and collected about 40 cans. Then we set off to get petrol from outside the city, but we could not get out because all roads were blocked. This was about four o'clock in the morning, so we had to stop firefighting and do what we could by other means.

By nine o'clock the army had managed to clear some roads and reliefs started to roll in. I had stationed my pump to work from the river that runs under Pool Meadow and when the reliefs came, I took my crew to collect my pump. The road had been cordoned off because an unexploded bomb was about six feet from my pump. I had been jumping over the hole during the night, I did not realise what it was. So I attached some ropes to my pump and very, very gently towed it away. Was I sweating!

My next experience was on the following Tuesday, 19th November, when the heavy raids started on Birmingham. I was sent to a fire at SU Carburettors, Bordesley Green. We started work on the roof, and then the Senior Officer told me to come off the roof and work inside the building. I went back to my pump that was stationed outside Saltley College, to tell the operator to increase the pressure. I then went back to the building and that's when the fun started for me. I was walking down a glass-covered drive at the side of the factory,

when a bomb was dropped just inside the factory. The factory wall was brought down, with me underneath. I was trapped and started calling out, someone heard me and then they started to dig me out. After about an hour I was dug out and I knew my left leg was broken just above the ankle. I was taken to Ralph Road station and my leg was dressed for a fractured ankle. The ambulance arrived and I was placed on the stretcher, and the men started to lift me into the ambulance. Some more bombs were dropped nearby, and the crew didn't know whether to drop me and run, or lift me in. Eventually we started off. Going up Ash Road a bomb was dropped on some houses and we had to pull up. The driver reported that the tyres had been blown off, so we carried on to the first aid station at Bordesley Green on the wheel rims. Quite an experience!

At the first aid station I was examined, and the doctor said I had a badly bruised ankle and I was to report to my own doctor next morning. I was put down the shelter under the building, and a landmine was dropped nearby and I thought I was going to be buried again. Luckily, I wasn't. Once was enough for one night.

Next morning after the all clear I phoned the station for transport to fetch me back, and they had quite a shock when I spoke. I had been reported *Missing, believed killed*.

I went to my doctor and he said it may be broken, we will try it for a week. I went the next week, he sent me to hospital, X-rayed, and it was broken. I had walked about for a week on a broken leg.'


## ▨ SOLIHULL **WI** ▨

'A report written in 1945 described the war effort of just one Women's Institute:

"Looking back over the past six years the members of the Solihull Women's Institute are justly proud of their achievements during the war for all have given unstintingly of their time and energy in a voluntary capacity in many and various ways, this despite the fact that the majority of members have found it almost a full time job in attending their own household duties while younger ones were directed to part-time war work.

In the early days of 1939 the members concentrated on making

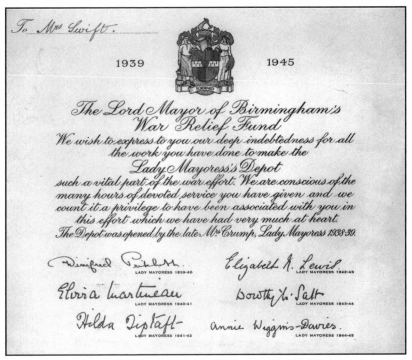

To Mrs Swift.

1939    1945

*The Lord Mayor of Birmingham's
War Relief Fund*
*We wish to express to you our deep indebtedness for all
the work you have done to make the
Lady Mayoress's Depot
such a vital part of the war effort. We are conscious of the
many hours of devoted service you have given and we
count it a privilege to have been associated with you in
this effort which we have had very much at heart.
The Depot was opened by the late Mrs Crump, Lady Mayoress 1938-39.*

Winifred ............
LADY MAYORESS 1939-40

Gloria Martineau
LADY MAYORESS 1940-41

Hilda Diplatt
LADY MAYORESS 1941-42

Elizabeth A. Lewis
LADY MAYORESS 1942-43

Dorothy L. Salt
LADY MAYORESS 1943-44

Annie Wiggins-Davies.
LADY MAYORESS 1944-45

*A thank you from the Lord Mayor of Birmingham in 1945.*

garments for the hospitals and making first aid post stretcher and
ambulance blankets and cushions. To enable wool and materials to be
purchased, a fund was started to which each member gave twopence
a week. This small fund was from time to time complemented by
proceeds from entertainments, sales and whist drives. Materials were
bought and a quantity of special gloves were made for men in mine-
sweepers. These gloves were specially cut and reinforced with string
fingers and palms to protect the hands when handling cables. Quantities of wool have been knitted into socks, scarves, gloves and hel-
mets for the Red Cross, prisoners of war, Navy, Army, Air Force and
trawlers.

The Institute has been a registered sub-depot for knitted garments
for the Royal Navy since the beginning of the war: 1,165 garments
have been completed, of which more than 50% were seamen's jerseys.

A large number of blue jumpers have been knitted for the WRNS and now children's garments for the liberated countries are being made. Fifty four hussifs have been sent for the women of the liberated countries.

The WVS has frequently been pleased to ask the help of the Institute members especially in organising the First Line Rest Centre. During the Blitz in 1940 and before the British Restaurant took over the feeding of evacuees a gallant band of WI members was responsible for the feeding as well as care of and sleeping of the evacuees on their arrival. The Institute has been opened on six occasions to receive people from blitzed areas of London and Coventry and again when there was an incident in the immediate neighbourhood.

On each occasion 80 to 100 people found refuge in the building for from four to five days at a time. During 1940 over 1,800 meals were served. The preparing and serving of these meals greatly taxed the ingenuity of the WI for members had to provide from their own homes most of the necessary cooking utensils. This was not easy as it was necessary to cook 25 pounds of potatoes at a time and other food in a like proportion, but members are proud of the fact that no one went away hungry and many of the children were introduced to milk pudding for the first time in their lives and liked it and asked for more!

Members have also been asked on two occasions by the Ministry of Health to run a demonstration opening of a rest centre to enable officials of other districts in the Midlands to see the methods so successfully employed at the Solihull WI.

The members have helped in the making of camouflage nets, 184 being completed. Racks were erected in the Institute and members donned overalls and worked hard and long at this very dirty and tiring work but the unpleasantness of the task was soon forgotten when it was realized how important these nets were to the Army.

Another activity at this Institute has been the operating of a Fruit Preservation Centre. Although this district is not classed as a fruit growing district approximately 1,500 pounds of jam has been made in three years from surplus garden fruit and sold to local retailers. Herbs have also been collected and dried and sent for inclusion in Red Cross parcels for prisoners of war.

The children have not been forgotten for at Christmas time the members have made thrift toys from odd scraps of material and sent them to the Red Cross and to the children at the Hermitage Home.

Members are proud of the fact that during the war the entire female staff of the local CAB has been composed of Solihull WI members, also the Chief Salvage Officer is an Institute member.

Many members have been doing nursing duties at the various hospitals, some have spent each Saturday and Sunday operating machines at engineering factories, a number of members have undertaken the cleaning of blood transfusion apparatus each week. Members have saved over £12,300 through the Institute Savings Association and the funds of many war charities and local appeals have gained considerably by the efforts of the Music and Entertainment Group and from bring and buy sales, whist drives and handicraft exhibitions."'

## ◼ On the Land ◼

'In 1940 we came to live in Meriden, when I was 15 years old. I left school and went to work on the land. I started every morning at 6 am and helped with the milking, fed the calves and the cattle in the yards. After breakfast I worked in the fields, some days leading the front horse when the men were ploughing. In summer we would follow the binder which cut the wheat and barley, and stook the sheafs of corn to dry out for three weeks. In haymaking time I would load all the trailers while the men pitched to me. In winter it was potato picking, and when very cold I had to go out and cut the kale with snow on it to feed the animals. They were long days but it was open fresh air.'

'After spending some years working as shorthand typists in Birmingham my friend Joyce and I decided when the war started it was time to try something new. I had always been interested in farming and, although we had no experience, we thought the Land Army was a good way to get away from it all. So May 1941 found Joyce and I cycling from Sutton Coldfield to a farm near Henley-in-Arden which was to be our home for the next five years. It was quite a large farm

*Land girls were essential 'Home Front' workers, as here at Meriden, and were officially thanked by Queen Elizabeth in 1950 at the London parade.*

with a milking herd, sheep, cattle, pigs and arable. The farmer and his wife made us very welcome, although I think they had misgivings about employing two girls straight from the town to do the work. The first morning we were woken very early and told to go and help with the milking. No machines – all hand milking – and a cow looks rather large when you first sit under one, never having been nearer than seeing them in a field with a hedge in between.

We spent the first week "muck carting". I think the farmer thought he would break us in the hard way – he told us afterwards he did not think we would last a fortnight, but we managed to survive, in spite of aching muscles, blisters and bad backs. We were expected to do all the varied jobs on the farm and work alongside the three men already employed there. We had to take a lot of leg-pulling at first but they eventually accepted us and we got on really well with them.

At one stage we had two Italian prisoners of war working with us. They arrived each morning on a lorry from the local POW camp. Neither of them could speak a word of English when they arrived, so we were given the job of trying to interpret, which, as you can imagine, caused a great deal of fun. They were very friendly and said they did not want the war any more than we did. Never having been used to farm work, they were not too keen on that side of things, but would much rather spend their time singing. You could hear them from one side of the farm to the other, and I never hear *O Sole Mio* without thinking of them, they certainly made life much more entertaining. We missed them a lot when they eventually left, I often wonder what happened to them after the war.'

'Just fill in the form, put down "market gardening" and prefer to live at home. So on 14th June 1943 I was called up having volunteered for the Women's Land Army and reported to my first of many farms, some twelve miles away. This was run by a middle-aged childless couple who welcomed me with open arms and were kindness itself. Enormous suet pudding oozing with fresh fruit covering the largest meat dish I have ever seen and that was for four of us. Sponges, pastries, huge breakfasts, "beggin" in the fields morning and afternoon, wholesome teas, not to mention the suppers, but I would have swapped it all during those first few weeks for my home with all its

mod cons and telephone, and that lovely cushy 9.30 to 5 job with one and a half hours at home for lunch working as a solicitor's secretary.

You name it, I did it, and all for 38 shillings per 48 hour week, less a shilling stamp, 21 shillings board and lodgings, five shillings bus and train ride home, after a four mile cycle ride to the bus, and five shillings I gave to my mother each weekend.'

'One of my best memories is of life on the Packington Hall estate, Meriden, where I served as a land girl during the years 1948 to 1951. Norah, another land girl, and I shared a flat on the top floor of the Hall, which we both loved. From our windows we had wonderful views of the deer park, lakes, river, the church and the beautiful trees. We still keep in touch and reminisce. We felt two of a family of estate workers and received many kindnesses from everyone, including our employers the late Earl and Countess of Aylesford and their families.

It was a time of change, from wartime to peace, and so while still involved in the old style, new appliances and methods were creeping in.

The highlight for me was in 1950 when I was a lucky winner in the draw for the Warwickshire contingent of the Women's Land Army to attend the farewell parade at Buckingham Palace to meet Queen

Elizabeth (now the Queen Mother) our patron, on Saturday 21st October. What a great occasion that was. The day before, we had a rehearsal and we were put through our paces by the Irish Guards at Wellington Barracks. I'm sure they had their work cut out, training us female farm workers to march. March we did, and all went well on the day, and it was a sight to behold in London. Our uniform was of cream shirts, with green WLA ties, green V-necked pullovers, green berets (replacing the original fawn felt hats), fawn corduroy breeches and wool socks, and brown leather laced shoes. No overcoats for the parade. Later we went on to a service in St Paul's Cathedral and I remember being totally moved by it all. It was wonderful.

The Women's Land Army officially ceased on 30th November 1950, though most of us stayed on the land, as I did.'

# A Child's War

*Children's lives were disrupted, as many in the cities were evacuated out to the countryside and those in village schools found their numbers doubled overnight. A time of stress and anxiety, but also a time when friends were made that have lasted a lifetime.*

### ◈ At School in Wolverhampton ◈

'In 1939 I was living in Penn, Wolverhampton and attending Wolverhampton Girls' High School on Tettenhall Road. By September, I was due to go into the Lower Fifth, the year we began to work for School Certificate. Imagine our joy when a letter arrived from school to say that we could not begin term until there were enough air raid shelters for us! (We were too young and silly then, I suppose, to think of the suffering and tragedy that would ensue once hostilities began in earnest.) Somewhat mitigating our joy, however, was the arrival of book lists and lessons to be done at home – yards and yards of instructions, with dates by which completed work was to be forwarded. Needless to say, much of it did not get done, but my friends and I achieved capital School Certificates at the end of the next school year, in spite of the late start and sundry lengthy sessions in stuffy shelters, once the raids started. (Not that Wolverhampton ever had a *real* raid; what we heard mostly, usually at night, was "ack-ack" fire from Penn Common.)

We stalwartly put up with school dinners that became more and more repetitive and boring, but what did make our hackles rise was when one of the hockey pitches was dug up so that we could dig for victory. I well remember being sent off to hoe as a punishment for some misdemeanour. We did other work too, to help the war effort, such as pea-picking, out near Bridgnorth, along with a tribe of gypsies, who sang songs the like of which we had never heard before. At Christmas, because the Post Office was so short of workers, we became "sorters" and I was able to buy Mother a tea cosy as a Christmas present, with my wages. Fire-watching in the long summer holiday was expected of us, too, once we were in the sixth form, and my friend and I thought we had reached the height of sophistication when we were put on duty with the chemistry mistress and her husband, both of whom were renowed Communists! To our disappointment they didn't sit and read the *Daily Worker* or put bombs under our camp beds, but talked about ordinary things and really tried to put us at our ease.

Most of the school activities continued as in peace time: the school play (with the hall heavily blacked out), sports day, concerts, the poetry-speaking competition, hockey matches (lemons unobtainable for half time, alas), but one event in particular remains in my mind. It had always been the custom for the Lower Sixth to run a party for a class from a local junior school, but with the growing deprivations of war time, I know that ours was particularly well appreciated. We chose a junior school from the other side of Wolverhampton and gave of our all. We saved our rations and made cakes, biscuits were carefully stored, mothers parted with home-made jams and we bought and made as many little presents as we could. Those little things had a whale of a time, especially enjoying the tea, playing in the grounds and running amok in the gym. Their little faces were a joy to behold in those dark days. They were so thrilled that they asked if they could give us a concert before they went home, and we nearly wept when their husky little voices were raised in *The Holy City*.

School was our little world, by and large, and at first I suppose because we were young and innocent and unrealistically optimistic we never felt afraid. We sorrowed with our friends when their brothers left for the war and felt most indignant when "our" submarine, which we had adopted, was torpedoed. The captain, I remember, came to school and presented us with the ship's bell and it was always used for the beginning and end of lessons. I wonder if it still is? It was not, though, until the day France fell to the Germans, in May 1940, that the fact of war impinged. Mademoiselle Savanier, our much-loved French mistress, had tears raining down her aged cheeks all day, and when I went home my mother, too, was weeping. I think we all grew up a little on that day.'

## ▧ A LABEL, A GAS MASK AND A SUITCASE ▧

'Eleven o'clock on Sunday, 3rd September 1939. Two parents and two children sat around the wireless waiting for Neville Chamberlain's statement. We heard it in silence. We were at war. Then, "Right," said Dad, "collect your things; we must get you to the school bus by half past one." I think I was excited. I was to take a big step into the unknown for we had no idea where I might be sent for safety.

The double decker bus was waiting when we got to my Coventry school. I was duly ticked off the list, loaded my old cardboard case and dashed upstairs to see better where they were sending me. I overheard Napton or Stockton but neither of these meant anything to me so I opened my gas mask case, took out my emergency bar of milk chocolate and munched away happily, abandoning my fate to those in charge.

We stopped at the village of Stockton but my name was not called. The bus emptied at Napton school and we all trooped inside to be greeted by the most formidable group of ladies I had ever seen. These ladies then set about choosing which of us they wanted, just as they would choose cattle on market day. There was one elderly lady standing there dressed from head to toe in black. She had her hair scraped back into a bun and wore horn-rimmed spectacles. She filled me with

dread. I willed her not to choose me but of course she did along with two of my classmates for whom I didn't particularly care either. So this was to be my lot. Oh Mum, where were you?

This "dragon" turned out to be the kindest lady one could wish to meet. She took us to her farm, gave us a splendid tea and took us to our shared room with its shared double bed which overlooked rolling countryside. I was blissfully happy there for three months during which time I learned to call in the cows, roll milk churns, collect eggs and help in the dairy. I was to be bridesmaid to my aunt at Christmas and needed to return home but the lady in charge of the evacuees said that if I went back to Coventry, I could not return to the village. We never did get an explanation for this.

So I went home but not for long. Soon the air raids began and friends of my parents who lived in Leicester offered to look after my small brother and I. I packed my case again and was soon installed in another strange house but this time with small brother for company. Six weeks later Coventry suffered the November blitz. A stray land-mine found its way to Leicester and blew out one window and filled the sitting room with soot. Next morning my parents arrived looking absolutely haggard to tell us that our house had been bombed. They were greeted by our hosts with the news that they couldn't cope with landmines blowing out windows *and* Peter and I and would Mum make other arrangements for us.

My parents, one aunt, two great aunts and one great uncle all of whom had been bombed out on the night of the blitz had moved in with my grandparents who lived in a small two up, two down plus kitchen and outside toilet which was shared with the family next door. There was no water, no electricity and no gas. Two sets of bunk beds had been installed in the downstairs front room and people rolled in and out of these according to their home guard, air raid warden and special constable duties. Peter and I were introduced into this chaos but mercifully were rescued after a few days by another friend of my father who had family in the Black Country who would be pleased to help.

This was our third journey into the unknown. I was nine and realised that my parents had our best interests at heart but my four year old brother was beginning to show signs of stress. We duly arrived in Cradley Heath to join a family who did not speak the English we recognised but they were kind and made us welcome. I went to school there, not working very hard until the headmaster called me into his room and said if I didn't buck my ideas up and work as well as he knew I could I would end up punching holes in buckets for a living. My journey to school took me through alleys where they made chains and other metal products and whilst I was fascinated by the constant shower of sparks to be seen through the open grilles, I had no wish to spend my days punching holes or anything else in that line of work. So I settled down, won gold stars galore and then our welcome wore out and we were moved out once more.

It was back to the family nest again. Back to wondering if we would get the clean water to wash in or the top bunk to fall out of. Fortunately a family friend this time offered to give us a home and so we made our fourth wartime sortie, to Huddersfield. Our host was a former minister of our church and he, his wife and son and daughter welcomed us into their home and for the first time we really felt part of the family. We spent almost two years there, very much part of the church and community. Peter started school there and I passed my scholarship and looked forward to going to the girls' high school. This was not to be for "Aunt Eva" fell ill and we were on the move again.

My parents had found and part furnished another house but before we could move in an incendiary bomb got there first, rather sneakily down the chimney, causing so much damage that my parents were obliged to look for shelter once more. Of course there was no room for the children so we were packed off to Atherstone where the girls' grammar schools were evacuated. Peter came too and we started the rounds again. He was a problem child by now and I was a bit cheeky so I can understand why no one would put up with us for long. Eventually the local authority hit on the idea of separating us and he, poor child, went the rounds again whilst I was billeted at Atherstone Hall with eleven other girls and so began the most exciting time a girl could wish for.

Atherstone Hall was a mansion set in several acres of woodland. It was beautiful, a child's paradise. We climbed trees, gathered wild strawberries, and built a hide in a secret part of the grounds where fighting had taken place in the Civil War and where we had no right to be. We explored secret passages leading from the house to the church and nowhere in particular, and clambered up and down spiral staircases which took us into the main house where we roamed whilst the family was at dinner, testing the four poster beds and gliding around the ballroom floor in our wincey pyjamas and socks. We found our way on to the roof and crept about up there, coming down again into our dormitory by way of a thick rope we found up there, much to the delight and amazement of those who had no head for heights or want of adventure. These escapades came to an abrupt end when someone in the town spotted us, and reported us to the police. No one was in the least amused.

All good things have to come to an end and in 1944 when bombing had ceased in Coventry and my parents had found another house I was able to go home. Peter went home a year earlier as soon as my parents were settled in. He suffered no lasting ill effects and has gone on to a fine academic career. As for myself, I am in no position to judge what effect all of this had on me, but as I look back on this time of my young life I cherish the experiences that made mine a childhood to remember.'

'While my father was away from home, sitting high up on the cliffs above Folkestone reporting on enemy activity coming across the Channel, the local Newtown air raid warden, Bert Deakin, kept an eye on me and mother. He would make sure that we were locked up for the night and if there was an air raid warning would knock us up and get us out of the house. We didn't have a shelter but opposite the house were fields with large oak trees in the hedges.

I still have vivid memories of one particular night when we stood under those trees wrapped in blankets. The whole of the sky was lit up by numerous flashes and it was almost as light as day. We learnt later that Coventry had been badly damaged that night.

It wasn't all doom and gloom though. There was a small hut at the bottom of the lane where social events were held and fancy dress parades were a popular feature. These were usually linked to National Savings weeks. Salute the Soldier Week comes to mind, when I was dressed in my grandfather's First World War khaki tunic with Savings posters fore and aft and a cap made from a third poster. I think the prize was a half-crown savings stamp.

*Helping the land girl in the fields was always a pleasure.*

In order to provide care for those of us whose mothers were out at work, the school remained open during the long summer holidays and we spent days on the canal bank and going for walks and picnics. If it rained we painted pictures and made models of aeroplanes and tanks. Well, it was wartime!

To celebrate VE Day we had a parade round the school playground. White dashed lines had been drawn on the tarmac so that we knew where to march and we practised hard so that we looked very smart. On the day we were lined up in height order. As the tallest it was my job to lead the line round the painted route. I couldn't understand why the watching parents were laughing so much as we all took our marching seriously, until I turned a corner of the pattern and there at the end of the line, getting left further and further behind, was the smallest boy in the school dutifully stepping on every little white dash. He had taken the instruction to "keep on the lines" literally.'

## Living with Auntie

'As an evacuee I first met "Auntie" on April Fool's Day. I remember it well as she answered the door with a broken chamberpot in her hand, she said it was because we'd startled her knocking on the door, but then we went in and had a cup of tea and the biggest slice of cake I'd had in my nine years, and what's more she offered me another slice which being a "greedy guts", I accepted. At home we only ever had one of everything and if there was only one item it was shared

three ways so that my brother and sister were equal with me. My brother and sister eventually came to live at Auntie's with me and then the trouble started and the example that sticks in my mind most of all was lumpy porridge.

Auntie used to make this at night and put it in the oven at the side of the fire so it was a thick lumpy concoction by the time we came to eat it. As we weren't allowed to leave the table unless we ate everything we were given, my brother and sister used to leave the lumpy bits and put them on my plate when she wasn't looking. I couldn't protest in case we got punished by sitting on the settee with straight backs. (That could be why I don't eat porridge anymore.) At dinnertime we had to eat all our dinner and the gravy because the pudding was put on the same plate and although we were lucky to have pudding and custard, cabbage and gravy didn't really mix.

But this mode of living did us good and when we went home for holiday Mom said it was unbelievable how we cleared our plates and ate everything that was put in front of us.

At the little village school there were only three classes – senior, junior and infant, so I was only ever in Mrs Baker's junior class. During this time the Americans used to drive through the village in convoy. We all used to stand at the school fence and shout, "Got any gum, chum?" One day one of the soldiers threw a box of sweets which I caught. It was a box of barley sugar, wrapped and so all the children lined up to take a sweet out of the box and guess what, there wasn't one left for me nor for my friend's sister. She was furious and much bigger than me and she pulled me round the playground by my plaits.'


⬧ IN LOCO PARENTIS ⬧

'At the outbreak of the war I was teaching in Birmingham – in a safe zone, although the school was within a stone's throw of a busy car factory. However, after Birmingham became a main target of the Luftwaffe it was decided the schools in the area should be evacuated. We went to Loughborough.

The children were excited; some had never been on a train! Parents were in tears as they waved goodbye. When would they see their

*Children were thanked for their part in the war effort by special Empire Day certificates.*

children again? Teachers accepted responsibilities – assuring parents that children would be well cared for. I saw one teacher in tears; she was leaving aged parents who depended on her.

We arrived in Loughborough, where the organization was excellent. Children were quickly allocated to volunteer families. Teachers (in twos) were sent to billets.

I hardly had time to settle when it was arranged that I should exchange with a teacher in Cheltenham who needed to return to Birmingham. I was happy and relieved as my elderly parents had just survived an enemy assault destroying houses near to them.

The Birmingham evacuees were at a junior school in Cheltenham. Life at school was interesting and stimulating. The evacuee children had adapted well, finding new friends and enjoying their new surroundings. They did not realise, at first, how long they would be separated from parents. Some parents visited frequently, but two children, a boy and girl (not related) had no visitors so needed my care.

What were my duties? I was in loco parentis so I made sure that children were happy and well cared for by the family with whom they were living.

I arranged expeditions – walks around Cheltenham to places of interest, the town hall where they tasted the spa water, the library, the shops, visits to the cinema. I inspected their clothes, notifying parents of their needs, or sending for parcels to the Lady Mayoress's Depot in Birmingham.

When the children moved to the senior school I moved too. This was a happy arrangement. Some children did not stay in Cheltenham for very long. Visiting parents took children back to Birmingham as they could not bear the separation.'

'For many inner ring Birmingham schools, evacuation took place on 1st September 1939. Parents had already given permission if they wished their children to go to a safe area, and so the exodus began. Imagine a long procession of children – infants and juniors from Dudley Road schools, walking down Winson Green Road to Winson Green station, to go by train, knowing not where journey's end would be. We all had our "possessions" with us, twelve children only to each teacher, or volunteer helper. Most children had brown paper parcels with them – hold-alls were unknown to these children. By the time we reached the station, I was carrying a few insecure parcels and my own small case. I doubt if any of my children had ever been on a train, so it was an "adventure" to them. No tears from the children, but weeping mothers waved goodbye.

Our carriage was for twelve children and Teacher – no corridor – but eventually we arrived at Stourport-on-Severn, and waited in the sunshine for the next move, the children quite happy seeing the green grass of the fields, and sitting on it. Gradually, the children were allocated to waiting foster mothers, and departed to villages in the area – Abberley, Astley, Bewdley, Dunley.

I think I thought at that time we would return to Birmingham within a few days. On 3rd September 1939 I knew otherwise, although I was unaware of the declaration of war until much later in the day – too busy making out labels, taking them to cottages for children to wear round their necks, name, address, etc and strict instructions to foster mothers "They must wear them all the time."

## Strengthening the room

If your refuge-room is on the ground floor or in the basement, you can support the ceiling with wooden props as an additional protection. The illustration shows a way of doing this, but it would be best to take a builder's advice before setting to work. Stout posts or scaffold poles are placed upright, resting on a thick plank on the floor and supporting a stout piece of timber against the ceiling, at right angles to the ceiling joists, i.e. in the same direction as the floor boards above.

How to support a ceiling

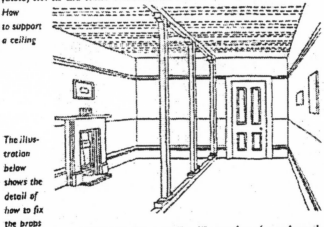

The illustration below shows the detail of how to fix the props

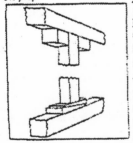

The smaller illustration shows how the posts are held in position at the top by two blocks of wood on the ceiling beam. The posts are forced tight by two wedges at the foot, driven in opposite ways. Do not drive these wedges too violently, otherwise you may lift the ceiling and damage it. If the floor of your refuge-room is solid, such as you might find in a basement, you will not need a plank across the whole floor, but only a piece of wood a foot or so long under each prop.

*Page 17*

*Advice from the Home Office in 1938 – a page from 'The Protection of Your Home against Air Raids'.*

By the end of September, the head of the infants school had been back to Birmingham, organised desks for all age groups, books, blackboards, pictures, everything to make some semblance of a school. The nursery wing of Dunley Manor – two rooms upstairs – that was to be "our school". Yes, you may have guessed. The head teacher returned to Birmingham, and left me in charge.

I became teacher, School Nurse, Caretaker, Firelighter – in fact general dogsbody – there was no one else to do the jobs, so I got on with it.

In February 1940 I managed to return to Birmingham, not to teach in our school, but home teaching in the front room of a house nearby. No more than twelve children together, as no air raid shelter had been built.

"Our" school had been a decontamination centre from the beginning of the war, and has never been a junior or infants school since. I had no family commitments in Birmingham, so went to the Education Office and volunteered to go on evacuation, to replace a teacher who needed to get back to Birmingham. I had six weeks in South Wales in 1941, then in spring 1941 began three years in Leicestershire, with Dartmouth Street and Bristol Street infants and juniors – they were considered the poorest schools in Birmingham 50 years ago. I have many memories of those years – never a dull moment!'

## ◩ A Silent Prayer ◩

'Like so many city children I was evacuated in September 1939. I was first taken to a stately home with seven other children. The lady of the manor was most shocked to be told that one child said she had a bathroom. This child also had a red dressing gown and the lady felt this child had to be seen to be believed. I well remember being escorted by a maid along a corridor and into a bedroom containing a four poster bed and having to stand on a long stool to speak to the lady. By the time I had finished telling her my life story we were great friends but she still thought the bathroom story was "made up". People who lived in Birmingham did not have bathrooms.

After three months I was sent to the next village and taken to live with a family in a farm labourer's cottage. One of my most poignant memories is of April 1940. My father had been an airman prior to the war beginning and I was told I could have the afternoon off as he was coming on the bus to see me. He duly arrived and I can still feel the excitement as we walked hand in hand past the village school, everyone looking at us as even then uniforms were not that familiar in the village. We walked down Catkin Lane and the catkins were hanging from the trees. I showed him the village pond and farm. We had tea and I went with him to the top of the village to see him off. We came to a crossroads and he said, "Don't come any further." He picked me up and kissed me and started to walk. At this time a lorry came by and stopped and gave my father a lift. He hung out of the window and waved and blew kisses to me as I stood there. That was the last time I would ever see him as on the 17th June the ship he was travelling on was torpedoed and 3,000 military personnel and nurses lost their lives.

I still go back after more than 50 years to my "second family" and often I stop the car at that crossroads and get out and once again I can see a fair haired little girl waving and blowing kisses to her father. This is when I say a silent prayer for all men and women who paid the ultimate price and left so much behind.'

# Highdays & Holidays

# MUSIC, DANCE AND CINEMA

*In our homes radio was king, but there were so many other forms of entertainment to be supported, from local sports to the weekly dance. Many of us went to the cinema every week, and how evocative of the past those 'picture palaces' are.*

## ▨ OUR FIRST RADIO ▨

'I was standing at the garden gate, about 1922 or 1923, with my father and a friend of his. This man was relating how he had heard someone speaking from London. I didn't know where exactly London was, only that it was a very long way off, and I thought what a very loud voice the speaker must have had. It was many years before I realised that my father's friend had been describing an early "wireless" broadcast.'

'Our wireless set, which was one of the first, had a horn to amplify the sound. The aerial had a power-breaker which was used during thunderstorms!'

'The First World War had ended and I was growing up in a new world with lots of exciting new inventions coming along. The one that stands out in my memory most of all was radio, or wireless as it was then called. I remember our neighbour had a crystal set and it was with awe my brother and I were allowed to don the earphones to "listen in". Later my father, with the help of a friend, built our first wireless set. It was very complicated with wires, terminals, valves and knobs packed into a very large wooden box. The loudspeaker was a separate affair. I remember a tree was felled and put up in the garden to which the aerial wire was attached and connected to the set in the house.

Power was via a large flat battery and a "wet" battery called an accumulator. This accumulator had to be recharged regularly at the nearest garage. They were horrid things, having acid inside so you had to be very careful not to spill any.

When the work was completed we all stood around the set with bated breath for the first sound from our wireless, which proved to be a great improvement on the old crystal set. My brother and I had to keep very quiet while the news was on and I recall church services on Sundays, Henry Hall's Band and of course *Children's Hour*. We joined the BBC Radio Circle Midlands which entitled us to have birthday wishes sent out over the air.'

## ▣ MUSICAL MEMORIES ▣

'Sixty years ago I was a relief pianist playing at a cinema in Walsall. My job was to supply the music for silent films, suiting the tempo to what was appearing on the screen.

I had launched into creepy music when an enormous rat jumped onto the piano, ran across my hands, then sat on the music stand looking at me! I was terrified but what could I do? If I had shrieked and panicked I would have emptied the cinema and incurred the wrath of the manager. I gritted my teeth and played on. By now the music had appropriately turned to "hurry music".

Another amusing experience occurred while I was nursing at a mental hospital. Of course I had to play the piano for any function they held. On this occasion I was playing at a dance for the patients. I had a drummer to assist me. At the end of the dance the staff and patients all stood up, ready to sing the National Anthem. My attention must have wandered. The drummer produced a roll on his drums, unfortunately this roll was identical to that which introduced the daily grace at meals.

Instead of playing *God save the King* I launched into the *Old Hundredth* and played "Be present at our table, Lord". I was mortified at the confusion which followed. The patients all thought they were getting a meal, but the Matron was definitely not amused.

Many years later, during the Second World War, I was still playing for dances accompanied by my sister-in-law. One dark night during the blackout we were making our way to Great Barr Hall to play at a dance for American soldiers.

We decided to take a short cut across the top end of Merrions Close; we were unaware that a wooden fence had been erected across the road. We walked straight into it, cutting our heads and bruising our faces.

We had to pass the isolation ward at the hospital in the Hall grounds, there we were bandaged and put to rights before we made our way to the Hall.

What a strange pair we made. A pianist with a bandaged head and only one eye visible and an accordionist with a black eye and a dirty face, but I've no doubt the Americans still enjoyed their dance.'

'My father was a musician in the orchestra at Her Majesty's Theatre in Walsall – a cinema now stands in its place – and he would get complimentary tickets for us. The tram ride up to the theatre was an experience in itself. Then we would sit in the front row of the stalls so that we could see my father playing the clarinet in the orchestra. I must have been quite young at the time, but I remember the shows and the marvellous atmosphere of the theatre. An added bonus was that my mother was occasionally allowed to take us backstage after the show.

At the top of the street where we lived was a magical place called Caldmore Green (very different now). We had our own cinema, The Forum, where I used to go every Saturday afternoon to see another instalment of *Flash Gordon*, starring Buster Crabbe – a wonderful specimen of manhood – who would be within inches of death at the end of every film, but thankfully still be alive for the following week's performance.

As I grew a little older, my friends and I would hold concerts in the yard at the back of my parents' house. We would imitate stars of the silver screen, and I would dress up in my eldest sister's clothes and perform impersonations of my favourite stars – like Deanna Durbin, Rita Hayworth and Jeanette McDonald – amid much fun and laughter. We made seats out of bricks with a plank laid across them for our audience, and charged ½d entrance fee. This fee included refreshments, which consisted of a large jug of lemonade (made from

Eiffel Tower crystals) served with broken biscuits. Everyone had to behave or risk being made to leave; this was not always easy, since some of the girls had to bring along their small brothers or sisters.

And then came my late teens, and for me the highlight of the war years was going dancing at Walsall Town Hall with my sisters. How well I remember the GIs coming from Lichfield in their covered trucks every Thursday and Saturday to attend the dance. When I first saw them leaping from their trucks, I thought they had come straight from Hollywood with their Yankee twang and chewing gum! We were really knocked out by seeing the jitterbug performed for the first time, to the sound of the big bands.'

## ◈ A NEW ERA ◈

'The advent of the silent films began a new era in everyday lives. People flocked to see them but were disappointed when, sitting enthralled at the serial, the caption "To be continued next week" was shown on the screen. The Saturday afternoon performance was for children; admittance was one penny, with sometimes a comic given free, albeit an out of date one.'

## ◈ MAKING ENTERTAINMENT ◈

'Knowle boasted a cinema. It showed films which had done the rounds so frequently the reels broke down but the audience was quite tolerant. The cinema had a corrugated iron roof so when it rained it was difficult to hear the soundtrack. There was an American army base at Knowle and the soldiers were fascinated by our "picture house" and many photographs were taken and sent back home to the States.

Knowle's bus service was not very frequent and there were not many cars around at that stage so our entertainment had to be made by ourselves. We had flourishing cricket and football teams, Guides, Scouts, Brownies and Cubs groups, Women's and Men's Institutes, Buffalos and church groups, the Girls' Friendly Society, the Mothers' Union and so plenty went on. In 1945 a youth club was formed, offering dancing, handicrafts, woodwork, discussion groups, table tennis,

*Tennis was popular in the 1930s and the Swift family of Birmingham had their own court.*

cricket and drama for young people. Many talents were discovered and life partnerships and friendships were formed.'

## ▨ FILMS, PLAYS AND OPERA ▨

'Cinemas proliferated in Coventry during the 1920s. I saw the first "talkie", Al Jolson in *The Singing Fool* and shed tears over "Sonny Boy" (previously reserved for the Gish sisters in *Broken Blossoms* and *Orphans of the Storm* at the Grand, Foleshill. The cinema in the heart of town was the Empire in Hertford Street, which had a flight of steps at the front – a favourite meeting place. As well as "the pictures" it offered the occasional "Flying Matinee", featuring famous performers and I saw Anna Pavlova dance there one afternoon.

There were two theatres, both in Hales Street. The Hippodrome catered for the popular taste in music hall and revue. I expect all the regular turns appeared but I only remember seeing posters for "The Tower of London, featuring Gracie Fields" after the war. The New Hippodrome (Coventry Theatre) was built and all the leading companies for drama, opera and ballet visited the city, whilst the annual pantomime always featured one of Britain's top comedians.

The Opera House provided different fare. Sometimes we had a musical (I saw *No, No, Nanette*) or opera (the Carl Rosa Company) but more often "straight" plays performed by the old stock companies, led by actor-managers, such as Frank Benson with Shakespeare plays (we were taken from school) and Fred Terry and Julia Nielson, his wife, in costume drama, such as *Sweet Nell of Old Drury* and *The Marlboroughs*. But the best entertainment ever provided in Coventry came when the Opera House was refurbished and a resident repertory company took over. We had a magnificent variety of plays. It was said the company read one play in the morning, rehearsed another in the afternoon and performed a third in the evening (twice!). When did they ever find time to forget one? This was remarkably good training for an actor, as members of the company like Phyllis Calvert, Gladys Spencer and Richard Chamberlain were to prove. I doubt if we appreciated our good fortune, whether we were regular first house Thursday patrons or paid 7d for a seat in the "gods" on Saturday nights.

Amateur acting of a very high quality was also a feature of the city's life in these years. The annual Gilbert and Sullivan opera with artistes like Arthur Sill, Walter White, W W Cheshire, and Marjorie Smith, was produced by the amateur operatic society; whilst the amateur dramatic society (one remembers Clara Salmon, Delia Morley, Gladys Cutler, Madge Lovell) offered us excellent productions of *Diplomacy* and drawing room comedies. We were a bit short on classical music; after all, the only hall big enough for an orchestral concert was the Drill Hall and I don't remember anything more than a recital by two or three of Britain's leading singers – Norman Allin, Walter Widdop etc. Regular concerts at the Methodist Central Hall,

TOWN  HALL  -  -  -  BIRMINGHAM

THURSDAY SYMPHONY

# CONCERT

29th November, 1951, at 7 p.m.

CITY OF

## Birmingham  Symphony  Orchestra

(*Leader:*  NORRIS STANLEY)

*Conductor:* RUDOLF SCHWARZ
*Solo Pianoforte:* MYRA  HESS

───────── PROGRAMME SIXPENCE ─────────

however, were an attraction and always included a performance of Handel's *Messiah* with Isobel Baillie as a soloist.

We enjoyed quality in our entertainment, even without taking the train to Birmingham, which was quite near and much more sophisticated.'


## ❖ Ghosts of the Past ❖

'Passing the boarded up, derelict Lyric cinema building, in Coventry's Holbrook Lane, I half expect to hear the ghostly laugh of Woody Woodpecker echoing through the barrel of barricaded doors at the front.

I call to mind its smells, the sound of the film reel, the smoke on the huge beamed spotlight that came out of the ceiling to project the film on the screen, and the uproar if it ever broke down. And the weird feeling, after we'd sat in the darkness of an afternoon, to come out into the daylight and find everything still the same, as the magic slowly evaporated out in the street.

Once inside, the whole thing was an experience. Used to wall-to-wall lino at home, the plush red carpet, with the gold edges, felt good, as did the huge anteroom, as big as three spare bedrooms, with settees nobody ever sat on; such a waste, I used to think.

You could go in at any time, and see the films through more than once if you wanted to. We all seemed to have more time to waste, then. There were two films usually, and lots of Forthcoming Attractions, which turned out to be a shadow of what had been promised.

You were shown in by the dancing torch of the usherette, and groped your way along the row to tuts, and sorrys, and thank yous, never quite sure of where the seat was till you arrived at it, as she often withdrew the torch before you were seated.

The screen would be covered between films with heavy velvet curtains, then ruched net curtains, then filmy gauze, and it would striptease its way into view, with the Pathe News cockerel, or the J Arthur Rank gong, or the lion with very healthy teeth and gums, and always, boringly, the British Board of Film Censors, which held the whole programme up. Plus, of course, Woody Woodpecker.

In those days, if we didn't like what was on at the Lyric, we could swiftly take ourselves off to the Regal (which was far from it) in the General Wolfe to see what was on offer there, or the Roxy just over Courtaulds bridge, or the Ritz, through at the bottom of Windmill Road, all within easy distance when you are a teenager, with energy in arms and legs and somebody to flirt with on the way.

Equally, if in town, it took only minutes to run from the Alex, (where I'd've like to have sawed down that round pole I sometimes got stuck behind, only it was holding the circle up) to the Gaumont up the hill, or the Empire in Hertford Street, or the Opera House in Hales Street, with its eerie upper circle cordoned off and its penchant for horror, or supernatural films.

There was also a cinema in Gosford Street, which was burned down, and one in Primrose Hill Street.

The Savoy was also a firm favourite, (not least because there was a sweetshop next door). It was not all carpeted, so a Malteser rolled from the back of the cinema made a lot of noise travelling down the slope to the front of the screen. Kids love to cause a commotion!

It seemed like the end of the world to me, on the day we arrived at the Lyric and the price had gone up to one and threepence – which of course, we didn't have. It was always my ambition to go upstairs, where I was convinced they saw a different film, in the one and nines. Sadly, when I became that well off the price had gone up.

I'd squeeze myself into a double seat with my friend Maureen, ready for the day I would sit that close to someone of the opposite sex, sort of practising. I suppose that's what you'd call it, too, in the interval when we strutted our stuff round the aisles, straining hooped starched petticoats, to see who'd noticed us, when the lights went up, and if someone said, "Come and sit here" we did, with the naivete of youth! Yet, somehow, it was safe then, everyone knew the rules, and nice girls didn't – not when the lights were on, anyway!

Yes, in those days, it was a fairy tale world where anything could happen, when, in our young eyes, romance might come our way. You had to be older for that, though, and sitting on the back row.

I remember the beautiful ice cream seller in the advertisement, with her gleaming smile and kindly countenance, who said in a Ruth Madoc voice, "Confectionery and ice creams available in the foyer of this theatre". Our ice-cream seller was about 60 with a wart in the corner of her chin, by her nose, and a powerful backhand for kids who tried to steal her wares. Kia Ora came in waxed cartons and one flavour, orange. Sometimes we chewed the wax pretending it was chewing gum, and we always indulged in a good few sucks of the empty carton, till an adult spoke to us severely about stopping.

Generally though, we kept a low profile, as it was possible that we could have paid for a cheap seat at the front, and then moved back, after the usherette had clipped our tickets. If we were challenged, we would cast round in the darkness for tickets we didn't have.

I remember seeing our teacher, Miss Heron, in there with a man, and we plagued her terribly, till she dropped her envelope bag and a Helena Rubenstein lipstick rolled on to the space at the front. The man fetched it for her and her glare of fury told us we'd be spoken to later! Somehow, it hadn't occurred to us that teachers were human, that they went to the pictures to see things like *Rock Around the Clock*!

Oh yes, I could get lyrical about the old Lyric, and sad at the passing of the small local cinemas.'

# SPECIAL DAYS

*Royal days were eagerly celebrated, from coronations to jubilees, in towns and villages all over the West Midlands. To travel to London in the 1920s was quite an event in itself, but when it combined a visit to the Empire Exhibition, it provided memories that have lasted over 70 years.*

### THE BRITISH EMPIRE EXHIBITION 1924

'On 14th June Syd took me for a day's excursion to Wembley. We went with the Daimler Motor Company's staff and Syd took me as a birthday present. I got up at 5.30 am and met Syd just after 6 am. We went to Coundon Road station to catch the 6.35 am train which was 20 minutes late. We had a very comfortable journey and arrived at Wembley Hill just after 9 am.

We walked through the Palace of Industry immediately upon our arrival. It was an enormous place and very, very interesting. I could have spent a whole day walking through there. We then went through the Palace of Engineering, which was the largest concrete building ever built. Finishing that we went across to Canada. This colony, I think, was one of the most interesting and beautiful exhibits there. There were models of the Niagara Falls, Rocky Mountains, wheat and farm areas and hundreds of other exhibits. I thought it was absolutely splendid.

At 11.30 am we went to the Popular Restaurant. Daimler had booked the whole place and I should think that about 500 sat down to lunch.

Afterwards we went into several of the colonies, such as Burma, Australia, The Government House, Hong Kong. They were very good, but I cannot remember many of the details to put down. At 2.30 pm we wended our way toward the stadium to see the famous Rodeo. The stadium was a huge place, and there were 80,000 people in it. This was the first performance to be held of the the Rodeo. It was very exciting, and the performance lasted over three hours. I was rather tired standing in the heat of the sun for that time. The weather was absolutely lovely, and very hot. When we came out people were queuing for tea so we did not attempt to get any.

Taking a break at the Pageant of Birmingham in 1938.

We visited the remainder of the other colonies. In Australia Syd bought me some apples and we sat down and rested there. The apples and fruit areas shown in this colony were lovely.

We then visited the Palace of Arts. In here were models of various buildings, model homes, etc. The Queen's dolls' house was exhibited here. We went in to view it, but were only allowed to walk round, not stop and study it because of the huge numbers of people there. From there we walked for an hour round the amusement park. We did not care to see any of the thrills or to go on the racer, scenic railway or any of the whirly things, but it was amusing to watch them. We then went into Canada again as I liked it so much and spent the remainder of our time looking round there.

Approaching ten o'clock we made our way slowly through the exhibition toward the station. I do not think I have ever seen so many people waiting for buses and trams in my life. The platform was absolutely crowded with people. At 10.55 pm the Daimler special came in. We had a lovely journey home. When we were about 15 miles outside London the light in our carriage gradually went out and we were left in total darkness. Needless to say, many people took advantage of such a calamity! We arrived at Coundon station toward

1.30 am and I reached home before 2 am on Sunday morning. This ended the day to which I had been looking forward to so long, and I think that the anticipation in this case was not better than the realisation. The day's outing was the loveliest birthday present I could have had and I shall never forget it.'


## ❖ ROYAL DAYS ❖

'The Royal Family seemed like fairy-tale characters to many people and in poor areas George V's Silver Jubilee in 1935 provided something to celebrate. Houses and streets were decorated and street parties were held. Sadly in 1936 George V died and the country went into mourning. The wireless broadcast bulletins about his health – the first time there was instant reporting.

As I had a great aunt living in America at the time my family were not surprised at the scandal of Edward VIII and Mrs Simpson and once again the wireless played a part. I can clearly remember Edward's abdication broadcast in December 1936. In May 1937 the

*The 1911 Coronation celebrations in Coventry.*

whole of the Coronation Service was broadcast – at least with the radio (as it was now called) you could move about doing things like getting meals. Once more the streets were decorated and people held street parties.'

## ▨ CORONATION DAY 1953 ▨

'We had a television for Coronation Day, the first in our road to do so. People living around crammed our house on the day to watch. Outside there were huge street parties, the funds for which had been raised by amateur concerts (excruciating!) and dances.'

'I was six years old in 1953. I did not really understand what all the fuss was about, except we had fun and a day off school.

*All dressed up for Coronation Day, 1953.*

**BERKSWELL**

# Coronation .. <br> .. Celebrations

## Saturday, June 6th, 1953

to be held in

### Berkswell Park

(by kind permission of
Capt. and Mrs. WHEATLEY-HUBBARD)

*Most towns and villages celebrated the Queen's coronation in 1953
with sports, games and food.*

Every Friday evening for weeks and weeks, Mrs Pamplin from the "outdoor" in our street, would come around and Mum would pay her one shilling. All mum would say was that it was for a street party.

The day before Coronation Day, we had a party at school and there was a fancy dress parade. Mum had spent many hours making me a bride's dress from paper doilies and crepe paper. We didn't have a sewing machine so Mum sewed it all by hand. Even my bouquet was made of red crepe paper roses. A real work of art. All Mum's hard work, however, paid off as I won first prize which was a musical box with the Queen on the front. I wore my hair in two long plaits at the time and I was never allowed to wear it loose but as this was a very special day, Mum allowed me to wear it flowing down. I felt like a real bride.

2nd June 1953 was a dull wet day from what I can remember. During the morning, I went to my friend Jacqueline's house because they were the first family in our yard to have a television. It was very crowded in Jacqueline's back room as all the neighbours popped in. We all ate sandwiches and watched this wonderful invention. It was all very exciting, especially for us children.

In the afternoon, our street party was held. As it was still raining, it was decided to put up the tables in a covered entry which belonged to one of the factories in our street. It was a huge entry and it was all decked out in red, white and blue streamers and balloons. A large trestle table laden with sandwiches, biscuits, cakes, squash and tea was in the middle of the entry and all the neighbours sat down together. There was singing, dancing and laughter and I found it very exciting. Now I understood why Mum had paid one shilling per week, it was for this wonderful party.

To round off the evening, Mum, Dad, my brother Christopher and I all went round to the local school where we carried on partying. My hair was still loose and I wore a white organza dress with a wide sash of red, white and blue ribbon. Christopher, who was only three at the time, wore a white shirt, blue trousers and red bow tie.

We danced and sang and I remember walking home, feeling very tired indeed, clutching my Coronation mug which we were given and which I still have today.'

# ALL THROUGH THE YEAR

*Every year brought its well loved pleasures, from winter wakes and old-fashioned Christmas celebrations to carnival time.*

## EARLSWOOD PLEASURES

'I went to Salter Street school when it was two rooms with open coal fires. In the summer there was always a May Queen and dancing round the maypole. On St George's Day the flag was flown in the playground and we all stood round singing all the patriotic songs, then went to the church next door for a short service and had the rest of the day off.

There were always two parties, one in the summer which was held outside and one in the winter in the village hall. Every child in the village came and we always went home with an orange, apple and a home-made pork pie which was given by Mr Cox who lived by the Red Lion. In the summer there were horse buses and landaus full of people from Birmingham coming for a day out to the lakes. A man called Mr Parrock ran pleasure boats on the lakes in the summer. In the winter they were frozen over and skaters came from everywhere to skate. There was always a man selling hot drinks and sausages which he cooked on a fire, made in a big oil drum with holes in the side and burning coke. The highlight of the year was the flower show which was held in the field opposite the Reservoir pub. It was always for the whole day with races for all the children and great competition for the biggest and best vegetables from all the men. Oh, for those lazy, hazy days of summer once again.'

## CARNIVAL QUEENS

'A carnival was organised every year in early October by the students from Birmingham University. The money collected was usually given to the hospitals in Birmingham.

*Carnival queens in the 1947 Birmingham carnival parade.*

I was one of the carnival queens in 1947. After riding in the Golden Coach through the city, in the afternoon we were taken to the Onion Fair. In the early evening we were introduced to the audience at the Aston Hippodrome, and ended up back at the Great Hall at Birmingham University for the Carnival Ball. It was a wonderful day and evening.'

### WINTER WAKES
'To our mining town in winter came the wakes, with all the fun of the fair. Families flocked to it, especially on Saturday night, and returned home with coconuts and cheap prizes they had won on the stalls.'

### CHRISTMAS BEGINS
'Christmas started for us about the end of November when grandmother visited us to make all the goodies for Christmas. She sat

*An organised bicycle outing could be a major expedition for the Powell family from Yardley during the 1950s.*

resplendent in a long white apron (her dresses were always black or navy blue) at the head of a large deal kitchen table. My mother, brother and I were assigned all the tedious jobs. We were lesser mortals for Granny had been a professional cook (a Mrs Bridges). We chopped nuts, de-seeded fruit (a very sticky chore done in a basin of warm water), grated carrot and sifted flour whilst she "expertly" did the mixing in a very large bowl – we were allowed a stir and a wish! Plum puddings, mincemeat and cake were all prepared this weekend, together with pickling onions and shredding red cabbage – a tearful task but we didn't mind for we knew Christmas Day was very near when this weekend came around.'

### ✦ No Lengthy Build Up ✦

'As children we loved Christmas Day. There was no lengthy build up, the majority of shopping being done during the week before. We didn't post cards until a day or two before Christmas and they were delivered on Christmas Day; a mince pie and a sixpenny piece were ready for the postman when he called. We usually had one main toy in our stocking and an orange, apple, nuts, new penny, coloured handkerchief, painting book and a few little novelties.'

## ❖ A Child's Christmas in the 1950s ❖

'I am lying on my back with my eyes open. The bedroom door is ajar and a thin wedge of light streaks on the far wall.

I can hear the muffled voices of my parents downstairs as they finish putting up the decorations. No discernible words, just changing tones through closed doors. My younger sister is in her bed beside me. Often she talks in her sleep, but tonight she is quiet. Her breathing is soft and the bedclothes move gently up and down.

We were going to stay awake. We talked until late but her speech became slurred as sleep overtook her. She will not see Father Christmas when he comes with our presents. I shall pretend to be asleep.

Downstairs on the dining room table we have put a mince pie and a glass of sherry. We know Father Christmas will need a snack to keep him going with all his work tonight. The reindeer shouldn't be left out either so we have left a carrot for them.

We collected Daddy's stockings from his dressing room. They are grey wool and darned at the toes. He wears suspenders to hold them up. Not like the pieces of white, knicker elastic which we use, but flat with clips and buttons like on our liberty bodices.

We were horrified to hear of friends who put pillowcases out instead of stockings. It seemed like terrible greed.

I am awake, but I must have been asleep. There is a weight on the

bedclothes at the bottom of the bed. I probe with my feet carefully so as not to topple anything onto the floor.

My sister is still asleep and I mustn't wake her. She'd want to open her presents and Daddy would tell us it wasn't getting up time yet.

When at last my sister wakes up we open our big presents together. Some are special to the time of year. Girl Annual for me and Robin Annual on my sister's bed, and the big Christmas present. Last year mine was a chemistry set and for my sister there was a large, furry fox with bright, glass eyes.

Other more ordinary presents which Mummy calls stocking fillers, are made special by being in the stockings. We feel them first. There are crinkly sounds from things wrapped in tissue paper, long thin things, and a scrunchy noise at the bottom, they are the nuts. It's lovely trying to guess what things are.

We take it in turns dipping into our stockings. First me, then her and we share each other's excitement. A painting book or a comic rolled into a tube, pencils, a rubber, marbles or jacks, streaky coloured rubber balls that bounce shoulder high, a tin of Barbola paste for modelling. We love the surprise of it all.

The traditional expectations are satisfied by the contents of the foot of the stocking. We know exactly what's going to be in it. Under a new hankie is a chunk of rocksalt, a symbol of good health, a shiny two shilling piece for wealth and a small lump of coal for good luck. And finally the tangerine.

When we come downstairs we look into the dining room. A few crumbs are left on the plate, the glass is empty and the carrot has gone. Sighs of relief. Our thanks have been acknowledged.

The soot in the hearth tells its tale, likewise the scrape marks up the chimney. We are satisfied. Christmas Day has begun.'

# Index

# LIST OF CONTRIBUTING INSTITUTES

*Contributions have been received from the following West Midlands Women's Institutes:*

Aldridge Afternoon ● Allesley Afternoon
Allesley ● Arden ● Barston ● Beacon ● Bentley Heath
Berkswell ● Bleak Hill ● Bourneville ● Castle Bromwich
Cheswick Green ● Dickens Forshaw Heath ● Dorridge
Eastern Green ● Four Ashes ● Great Barr ● Green Lane
Hall Green ● Hampton in Arden ● Harborne
Heart of England ● Hobs Moat ● Hockley Heath
Hodge Hill ● Hurst Green ● Keresley & Coundon
Keresley Newlands ● Kings Heath ● Knowle
Lode Heath ● Marston Green ● Meriden ● Monkspath
Newton ● Olton ● Packwood ● Park Hall ● Pelsall
Perry Beeches ● Quinton ● Sheldon ● Shirley ● Silhill
Solihull ● Solihull Evening ● Stechford ● Streetly
Sutton Coldfield ● Temple Balsall ● Walmley
Walmley Ash ● Walmley Evening ● Whateley Green
Wylde Green